D0084440

Let's Start Talking

Conversation for High Beginning and Low Intermediate Students of English

George M. Rooks

University of California, Davis

HEINLE & HEINLE PUBLISHERS

A Division of Wadsworth, Inc.
Boston, Massachusetts 02116

The publication of *Let's Start Talking* was directed by the members of the Newbury House Publishing Team at Heinle & Heinle:
Erik Gundersen, Editorial Director
Kristin Thalheimer, Production Editor

Also participating in the publication of this program were:
Publisher: Stanley J. Galek
Editorial Production Manager: Elizabeth Holthaus
Project Manager: LeGwin Associates
Assistant Editor: Karen Hazar
Associate Marketing Manager: Donna Hamilton
Production Assistant: Maryellen Eschmann
Manufacturing Coordinator: Mary Beth Lynch
Photo Coordinator: Martha Leibs-Heckly
Interior Designer: LeGwin Associates
Illustrator: Ruth J. Flanigan
Cover Artist: Rhonda Voo
Cover Designer: Bortman Design Group

Art credits:
p. xiv Barbara Alper/Stock Boston; p. 8 Fredrik Bodin/ Stock Boston; p. 18 Reuters/Bettmann Newsphotos; p. 30 Comstock; p. 35 Courtesy of Skelton-Morris Associates; p. 42 UPI/Bettmann (woman), Michael Goldman/FPG International (man); p. 50 Bob Daemmrich/Stock Boston; p. 60 Robert Brenner/ PhotoEdit; p. 72 William Johnson/ Stock Boston; p. 76 Courtesy of Rand McNally; p. 82 Spencer Grant/Monkmeyer Press; p. 90 Elena Rooraid/ PhotoEdit; p. 98 Cary A. Conner/PhotoEdit; p. 106 Hazel Hankin/Stock Boston; p. 114 Stewart Cohen/Index/Stock Int'l Inc.; p. 124 Dennis Hallinan/FPG International; p. 132 Peter Menzel/Stock Boston; p. 140 David Frasier Photolibrary (hotel lobby), Tony Freeman/PhotoEdit (phone bills); p. 146 Ray Atkeson/Monkmeyer Press; p. 156 Archive Photos (smokers), George M. Cassidy/The Picture Cube (physical fittness); p. 160 FPG International; p. 166 Gale Zucker/Stock Boston.

Heinle & Heinle Publishers is a division of Wadsworth, Inc.

Manufactured in the United States of America

Library of Congress Cataloging in Publication Data
Rooks, George M.
    Let's start talking : conversation for high beginning and low intermediate students of English /
George M. Rooks.
                                p. cm.
    ISBN 0-8384-4825-9
    1. English language—Textbooks for foreign speakers.   2. English language–Spoken English. 3.
Conversation.   I. Title.
PE1128.R6395 1994
428.3'4—dc20   93–41508
                                                               CIP

ISBN: 0-8384-4825-9
10 9 8 7 6 5 4 3

Contents

You are members of the Alaska Park Commission. What is best for Notaki State Park: oil drilling? gold mining? fishing? hunting? timber cutting? How do you decide among Eskimos, large companies, and other people? Identify the national parks in or near your area.

You are editors of Popularity Magazine. You must decide what or who is fashionable and what or who is not. What would you say about Madonna? men's earrings? Arnold Schwarzenegger? short skirts? Levi jeans? tattoos? Michael Jackson? cigarettes? Interview Americans about their ideas of what is "in."

The sun is about to explode. People all over the world are getting crazy. Should your family do nothing? see a psychologist? buy guns and food? take a vacation? Write a letter to your best friend about what you would do.

What would you rather do in the future: be ugly and happy or handsome/beautiful and unhappy? stay single or get married? win a Nobel Prize or make a lot of money? become president of your country or president of a large corporation? Write about your dreams for the future.

To Hila Rooks
for her patient listening and careful analysis
that have added so invaluably to the text

To the Teacher

Let's Start Talking was conceived of as a lower-level companion to the intermediate *Can't Stop Talking* and the advanced *The Nonstop Discussion Workbook.*

Continuing the tradition of *Nonstop* discussion, *Let's Start Talking* offers upper-beginning and lower-intermediate students an opportunity to express their ideas about stimulating problems in an interactive small-group setting. As with the previous books, the purpose of *Let's Start Talking* is to generate discussions and conversations in which the students do almost all the talking.

The structure of *LST* will be familiar to those teachers who have used the two earlier texts. Essentially, each unit includes the following sections:

1. Vocabulary: Important vocabulary is given and defined.

2. Read and Consider: The problem is described and points to consider are explained.

3. Decide and Write: Specific information is detailed and students are asked to make choices.

4. Prediscussion: Practical conversation phrases appropriate to the problem are given along with model conversation(s) and/or discussion(s).

5. Discuss: The students are directed to share their ideas orally.

6. Extend: A written/oral assignment and a cultural contact assignment based on the problem are suggested.

Suggested Use of Class Time for a Sample Unit (Unit 4)*
(based on a 50-minute class)

Day 1

Presentation of Situation (15–20 minutes)

Ideally, the teacher will have assigned parts of the unit for homework before class work begins. Specifically, the students should have thought about the photograph(s) and/or artwork, reviewed the vocabulary, and read the *Read and Consider* section. Whether the students are assigned the *Decide and Write* section and the *Prediscussion* section for homework is at the discretion of the teacher.

The teacher introduces the unit by discussing the unit title as well as the photograph(s) and/or drawing(s). For example, at the beginning of *Unit 4*, "How Will You Plan Your Family's Budget?", it is important that the students understand what a budget is. Time should be taken to explain *budget* and to apply the word to the students' lives—by asking them about their budgets. Moreover, the teacher might write her or his monthly budget on the board or solicit and write down such information from a student.

Before proceeding, the teacher should make sure that the students understand the situations that will be presented and the target vocabulary.

The teacher (or a student) then reads the entire *Read and Consider* section aloud while the students follow along silently. The teacher should make sure the students completely understand the situation and the considerations. After reading through the *Read and Consider* section at least once, it may be useful to pose some questions to the students concerning the reading to make sure that they have understood what was read. For example, in *Unit 4*, questions such as "What kind of family is it? Where does the family live? Who is in the family? Why do they need to move?" will reinforce the reading and help the students warm up.

Presentation of Choices (15–20 minutes)

If the students have been assigned the *Decide and Write* section for homework, the teacher should briefly review the choices with the students—clarifying any questions that the students may have and covering any difficult vocabulary. (If the students have not been assigned this section for homework, such clarifying and covering may take longer.) For example, in *Unit 4*, it may be necessary to go over Area 3: Medical Insurance, or Area 7: Car Insurance, with the class.

If the students have already written down their choices for homework, the class can proceed to the *Prediscussion* section: if not, at least ten minutes of class time should be allotted for students to make their individual decisions.

*Note: The following lesson plan cannot be used for all units because of the variety of formats and directions. In all cases, the teacher is encouraged to be flexible and creative in applying lesson structure.

Discussion Preparation (15–20 minutes)

The teacher should begin by introducing the suggested conversational phrases (in *Unit 4*, these include "Making Suggestions, Agreement, and Disagreement"). The teacher should read the phrases aloud and have the students repeat them.

Next, the teacher should pair the students and have them practice using the phrases. For example, one student might begin by being the "suggestion-maker" and the other the "agreer or disagreer" (after a few minutes, the students would reverse roles). The students should be encouraged to be as creative as possible in their practice. For instance:

> Student A: I definitely think that we should leave the class!
> Student B: You've got to be kidding.

Afterwards, the students should proceed to the model conversation(s)/discussion(s). In *Unit 4*, this will mean expanding the pair to a threesome.

In the models, each student should have the opportunity to play different roles in order to develop a better feeling for the phrases. In addition, the teacher should encourage the students to experiment with the phrases, substituting those in the models with others from the list(s)—that is, the students should not just repeat the exact words of the model each time. For example, in the long model discussion for *Unit 4*, the second sentence "I don't think that's a good idea because it's too small" could be restated as "That doesn't make sense because it's too small" or as "I'm not sure that's a good idea because it's too small."

Day 2

Discussion of Problem (Group Resolution) (30–50 minutes)

By this point, the students should be ready to address the problem, and the class should be divided into small groups—with particular attention paid to such issues as nationality, language, gender, and personality.

The teacher should encourage the students to consider the problem carefully and to reach a group consensus as to each aspect. In regard to *Unit 4*, additional time may be necessary due to the "multiple-discussion" nature of the *Discuss* directions.

While the students are discussing the problem, the teacher might walk through the class, answering any questions, listening to discussions, and resolving any difficulties. However, the teacher should try to be as inconspicuous as possible—allowing the students to bear the full responsibility for discussion.

Class Sharing (20 minutes)

If the discussion lasts for 50 minutes, "Class Sharing" can be done on the next day. One technique is to put a grid on the board and have a member of each group fill in the group's choices. Here is an example for *Unit 4*:

	Group 1	Group 2	Group 3
1. Housing			
2. Food			
3. Med. Ins.			
4. Elect.			

(and so on)

After the students have filled in their groups' choices, the teacher acts a moderator—pointing out significant similarities and differences and asking groups and individuals about their particular choices. If there is disagreement within a group, the teacher might ask group members to describe what other people in the group thought. In all cases, the teacher should encourage interchanges between groups.

Day 3

Extending (50 minutes)

The assignments in this section are designed to extend the issues beyond mere values clarification. The amount of time devoted to the assignments will depend upon the individual teacher.

For example, *Unit 4* activities include writing a budget and comparing it with those of classmates as well as looking at apartment advertisements in the classified ads section of newspapers.

Let's Have a Party!

Vocabulary

during   in

Read and Consider

You arrived in Urbana, Illinois, one week ago. You are new students in an English program. Your English program is great, and you have worked hard all week. Now you want to have some fun during the weekend. Your class is going to have a party.

All of your classmates will be at the party. They are friendly, but you don't know them very well. To meet one another and to plan the party, your class is going to play a conversation game.

Each person will have the same list of questions (see the *Decide and Write* section). During the next hour, you will use these questions to start conversations with your classmates.

Preconversation

Before you start each conversation, introduce yourself. Study the following introduction expressions. Repeat each one after your teacher. Then practice them with a partner. Fill in the spaces [. . .] with your name and your partner's name. Take turns introducing yourself and responding.

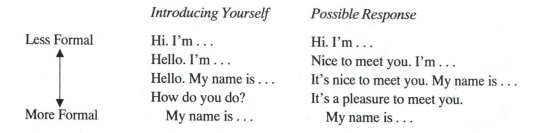

	Introducing Yourself	*Possible Response*
Less Formal	Hi. I'm . . .	Hi. I'm . . .
	Hello. I'm . . .	Nice to meet you. I'm . . .
	Hello. My name is . . .	It's nice to meet you. My name is . . .
	How do you do?	It's a pleasure to meet you.
More Formal	My name is . . .	My name is . . .

After you introduce yourself, you will have short conversations with each classmate. In each conversation, you will do the following:

1. Ask a question from the list.

2. Show interest and use a follow-up.

3. Pre-close the conversation.

4. Close the conversation.

Study the following conversation expressions. Repeat each one after your teacher. Practice them with your partner. Take turns showing interest and responding. Pause briefly at each [. . .].

	Showing Interest/Following Up	*Possible Response*
Less Formal	Mmm-hmm. . . . What about you?	Well . . .
	Uh-huh. . . . How about you?	Well . . .
	Interesting*. . . Tell me more.	OK . . .
	Really?*. . . Why? (or) Why not?	Because . . .
	You don't say. . . Could you tell me more about . . . ?	I'd be happy to.
More Formal	Would you mind telling me more about . . . ?	

*Often one word is used to show interest instead of a sentence or phrase. For example, "Interesting" instead of "That's interesting" and "Really?" instead of "That's really interesting" or "Oh, really?"

	Pre-closing the Conversation	*Possible Response*
Less Formal	OK . . . great talking to you.	Same here.
↑	Thanks a lot for the information.	No problem.
↓	Well, I'm afraid [it's time to	I think so too.
More Formal	change partners.*]	

	Closing the Conversation	*Possible Response*
Less Formal	See you later.	Take it easy.
↕	Talk to you later.	Bye.
More Formal	Good-bye.	Good-bye.

Read the following conversation. See how the conversation expressions are used. Practice the conversation with your partner.

(Two people)
A: So, what do you want to know?
B: Well, how about question 2: When's your birthday?
A: In March.
B: Mine too! What day?
A: The 5th. What about you?
B: The 17th.
A: Really? How old are you?
B: 27. How about you?
A: Well . . . I'd rather not say. Let's just say I'm older than you.
B: Come on. You can tell me.
A: Well, OK. I'm 38, but don't tell anybody.
B: Why not?
A: It's a secret.
B: Why?
A: It's personal.
B: OK, if you say so.
A: Well, I'm afraid it's time to change partners. We'll talk more next time.
A: Good.
B: Talk to you later.
A: Bye.

*In conversation, it is more common to say, "Well, I'm afraid I have to go."

Decide and Write

Stand up and walk around the room. Have a small conversation with each classmate; ask each person one question from the list. Afterwards, talk to your classmates again; ask them three questions from the list. Continue moving around the room and asking questions. Do not stop until you have filled in a name on each blank [_____].

    Write down the names of two classmates who:

1. have the letter "a" in their first name
   (How do you spell your first name?)

   _____

   _____

2. were born in December or January
   (When is your birthday?)

   _____

   _____

3. have more than two brothers and sisters
   (How many brothers and sisters do you have?)

   _____

   _____

4. like to dance
   (Do you like to dance?)

   _____

   _____

5. like rock music
   (What kind of music do you like?)

   _____

   _____

6. do **not** like to go to parties
   (Do you like to go to parties?)

   _____

   _____

7. usually go to bed after 1:00 A.M.
   (What time do you usually go to bed?)

   _____

   _____

8. smoke cigarettes
   (Do you smoke cigarettes?)

   _____

   _____

9. do **not** like to drink alcohol
   (Do you like to drink alcohol?)

   _____

   _____

10. like to eat junk food at parties
    (What kind of food do you like to eat at parties?)

    _____

    _____

11. are funny
    (Are you funny?)

    _____

    _____

12. like to play games at parties
    (What do you like to do at parties?)

    _____

    _____

13. are in love
    (Are you in love?)

    _____

    _____

14. have kissed someone at a party
    (Have you ever kissed someone at a party?)

    _____

    _____

15. have been to a good party recently
    (When was the last good party you went to?)

    _____

    _____

Discuss

When the game is finished, go over the answers with your class. Try to remember the names of all of your classmates and something interesting about each one of them.

Extend

Written/Oral Assignment

1. With a partner, write a "party" conversation between two people. In the conversation, the people should introduce themselves and ask questions about their native country, family, job, favorite activities, and other points of interest. Afterwards, role-play the conversation for the class.

Cultural Contact Assignment

2. Plan a real party with your classmates (the party can be inside your classroom or outside). Use the information from the conversation activity to help you. Decide what kind of food and drinks you will have and what kind of music and activities you want. When will the party start? When will it end? When you have finished planning, have a party!

Which Grand Prize Will You Take?

Vocabulary

contest   game

grand prize   biggest prize

offered   given

since   because

worth   valued at

limo   big car

luxury   something expensive

Read and Consider

Unbelievable! Nine months ago, a television station in Phoenix, Arizona had a contest. You and your best friends entered the contest. Yesterday, you received a letter from the television station.

You have won a grand prize! You will have one week to choose the best prize. Since you and your friends entered together, you all must agree on the best prize.

Decide and Write

Before you discuss your ideas with your group, read the choices carefully. Put the choices in order of your preference (1 = best, 9 = worst). Give a reason for each choice.

Prize 1: A new red Ferrari Testarossa and a new Rolls-Royce Silver Shadow
You will also receive $25,000 of free gasoline.

Ferrari Testarossa   Rolls-Royce Silver Shadow

Order: _____

Reason: _____

Prize 2: 50,000 free movie tickets
You can use these tickets anywhere in the world. You also receive one free Coke and one free bag of popcorn at each movie.

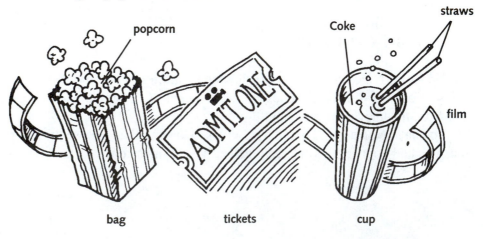

bag   tickets   cup

Order: _____

Reason: _____

Prize 3: **A 60-day trip around the world for 2 people (airfare + hotels)**
You will stop in Hong Kong, Delhi, Nairobi, Vienna, Stockholm, Buenos Aires,
New York, and Vancouver. You will also receive $100,000 in spending money.

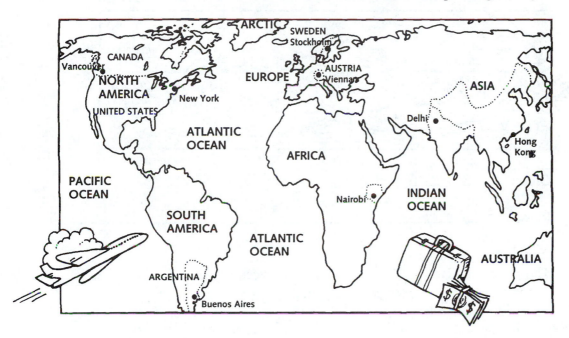

Order: _____

Reason: _____

Prize 4: **Five diamond rings worth $75,000 each**
Each ring contains one beautiful 10-carat diamond.

Order: _____

Reason: _____

Prize 5: **An island in the south Pacific ocean**

You will be the owner of a lovely island (43 sq. mi.). Nobody lives on the island. It is 200 miles away from any other island.

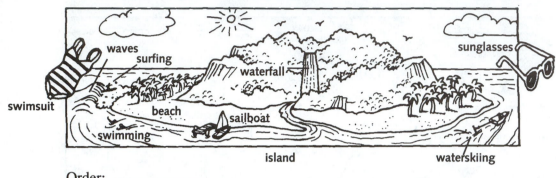

Order: _____

Reason: _____

Prize 6: **Free food for life**

This prize will give you $250 of groceries per week for the rest of your life.

Order: _____

Reason: _____

Prize 7: **An apartment in St. Moritz, Switzerland**

The apartment is beside the most beautiful mountains in Switzerland.

Order: _____

Reason: _____

Prize 8: **Chauffeur and maid service for the next ten years**
This prize gives you a limo, driver, and a live-in maid for ten years.

Order: _____

Reason: _____

Prize 9: **$275,000 in cash**

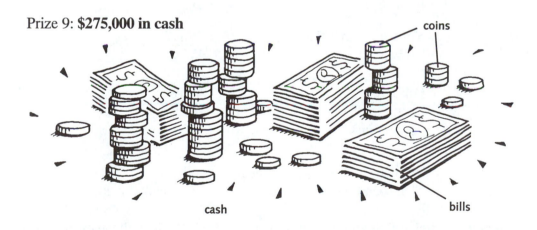

Order: _____

Reason: _____

Prediscussion

In this discussion, you are going to talk to your best friends. Your discussion will be very informal. You will either agree or disagree with your friends.

Study the following expressions. Repeat each one after your teacher. Then practice them with a partner. Take turns agreeing, disagreeing, and responding.

	Agreeing	*Possible Response*
Strong	Great idea.	OK! Let's (do it*)!
↑	Definitely.	OK! Let's do it!
	I agree.	OK, let's do it.
	Good idea.	OK, let's do it.
↓	I think so too.	OK, let's do it.
Not So Strong	That seems like a good idea.	You really think so?
	I guess that's a good idea.	You really think so?

	Disagreeing	*Possible Response*
Strong	You've got to be kidding!**	Why?
↑	No way.**	Why?
	I disagree.	Why?
	I don't think that's a good idea.	Why not?
↓	I don't think so.	Why not?
Not So Strong	I'm not sure that's a good idea.	Why not?
	That sounds good, but . . .	You really think so?

Continue practicing the expressions with your partner. Begin with the examples.

Example 1   A: I think we should take the cash.
B: Great idea!
A: OK, let's take it!

Example 2   B: I think the diamonds are the best.
A: I don't think so.
B: Why not?

*"Do" might be replaced by any appropriate verb—depending on the situation, such as "Let's see it!" or "Let's eat it!"

**"You've got to be kidding!" and "No way" are very strong and may be considered impolite in certain formal situations. They should be used with special care.

In conversations and discussions, people often do not understand each other. One speaker must ask another speaker to repeat. You may use the following expressions to ask a person to repeat. Practice these expressions with your teacher.

Asking for Repetition

Less Formal	Sorry, what was that again?
↕	I didn't understand what you said. Could you please repeat that?
More Formal	Excuse me, would you please repeat that?

Study the following discussion. See how the expressions are used. Practice the discussion with three of your classmates. Take turns being A, B, C, and D.

A: OK, group, what's the best choice?
B: No idea.
C: Me either. I think we ought to go down the list.
D: OK, but I'm voting for the Ferrari and the Rolls.
C: Sorry, what was that again?
D: I said that I think the Ferrari and the Rolls Royce is the best prize.
B: You've got to be kidding.
D: Why?
A: There's four of us and only two cars.*
D: We can take turns.
C: No way.
D: Why not?
B: How can you share cars?
D: Easy. One week you've got the Ferrari. Three weeks you don't.
A: That sounds good, but I don't think it would work.
B: Me either.
D: We already share an apartment. Why not cars?
B: Well . . . maybe. But speaking of sharing, what about the cash? We can always share money.
A: Definitely.
D: I still like the cars.
C: Well I still think we ought to go down the list.
A: Good idea.
B, D: OK, OK. Let's do it.

*Note that in discussions, anyone can answer a question—not only the previous speaker. Also note that statements are sometimes not grammatical. In informal spoken English, "there's four of us" may be used, but in formal spoken English and in written English, "there are four of us" must be used.

Discuss

Talk to your friends. Explain your opinions. Agree on a specific order. Afterwards, discuss your choices with the class.

Extend

Written/Oral Assignment

1. Write a letter to your best friend. In it, tell your friend about the contest and about the prize you chose. Explain why you chose the prize and what you will do with it.

Cultural Contact Assignment

2. Go to a supermarket. Find out how much the following items cost. Write down the cheapest cost for each item. Can you buy all of them for less than $250? Discuss your information with the class.

Food	Cost
5 lbs. hamburger meat	_____
3 gallons regular milk	_____
1 dozen AA eggs	_____
1 package spaghetti noodles	_____
10 lbs. potatoes	_____
2 lbs. cheddar cheese	_____
2 liters Coca Cola	_____
1 5 lb. jar chunky Skippy Peanut Butter	_____
2 loaves whole wheat bread	_____
5 lbs. flour	_____
1 whole chicken	_____
1 broom	_____
3 large cans corn	_____
3 large cans green peas	_____
10 lbs. rice	_____
2 heads lettuce	_____
6 rolls toilet paper	_____
2 large boxes Kellogg's Corn Flakes	_____
5 lbs. sugar	_____
5 lbs. bananas	_____
10 packages Top Ramen soup	_____
5 cans frozen orange juice	_____
1 pint ice cream	_____
2 packages margarine	_____
5 bars Palmolive soap	_____
3 large cans tomato sauce	_____
1 large Head & Shoulders shampoo	_____
1 large can coffee	_____
1 large bottle olive oil	_____
1 large box Tide detergent	_____
5 bunches broccoli	_____
1 box napkins	_____
TOTAL:	_____

What Songs
Can We Write?

Vocabulary

a hit   something very popular

perform   to present

make sense   to have meaning

Read and Consider

You work for the Delta Delta record company in Miami, Florida. During the last two years, your company lost money. None of Delta Delta's songs was a hit.

You have one last chance to save your company. Whitney Houston will sing one song about love; Guns N' Roses will sing one rock song, and a new band, Legs, will perform one rock or love song.

You, the songwriters at Delta Delta, have to write the songs. Each song must have at least 20 lines.

Prediscussion

Turn to the *Decide and Write* section, and look at song 1. Then turn back to this page.

In this discussion, you will be talking about the words to songs. Study the following conversation expressions. Repeat each one after your teacher. Then practice them with two partners. Take turns saying something sounds good or not good, agreeing, and disagreeing.

Saying Something Sounds Good	*Agreeing*	*Disagreeing*
That sounds good.	I think so too.	I don't (think so).*
Sounds good to me.	To me too.	Not to me.
I like the way that sounds.	Me too.	
	So do I.	I don't.
I think that sounds pretty good.	I do too.	

Saying the Meaning is Clear		
That makes sense.	I think so too.	I don't (think so).*

Saying Something Doesn't Sound Good	*Agreeing*	*Disagreeing*
That doesn't sound good/right.	I don't think so either.	I do (I think it does).
		Yes, it does.
Sounds strange to me.	To me too.	Not to me.
I don't like the way that sounds.	Me either.	I do.
	Neither do I.	

Saying the Meaning is Not Clear		
That doesn't make sense.	I don't think so either.	I do (I think it does).
		Yes, it does.

*The disagreement response differs slightly—depending on the position of the disagreement in the discussion. For example:
A: That sounds good.
B: I think so too.
C: I don't. (This statement directly responds to "I think so too.")

A: That sounds good.
B: I don't think so.

People in small discussion groups are often shy about giving their opinions. The following expressions can be used to ask a person about his or her opinion. Repeat them and practice using them with your teacher.

Asking for an Opinion from Your Classmate

Well, what do you think?
What's your opinion?
How do you feel about that?

Continue practicing the expressions with your two partners. Begin with the examples.

Example 1   A: I like the way that "love" sounds.
B: Me too.
C: I don't.
B: Why not?
C: It's not a romantic situation.
A: That's a good point.
B: Yeah, I see what you mean.

Example 2   A: "Love" doesn't make sense.
B: I don't think so either.
C: I do.
A: Why?

Example 3   A: "Love" doesn't make sense.
B: —
C: —
A: Well, what do you think?
B: I don't think it makes sense either.
C: Me either.

Study the following discussion between three people. See how the expressions are used. Practice the discussion with two partners. Take turns being A, B, and C.

A: What word's the best in line 1?

B: I think "like" sounds pretty good.

C: Me too.

A: Well, I don't.

C: Why not?

A: Have you ever been in love?

C: Just once.

A: Did you ever say, "I will always like you"?

C: I see what you mean. "Like" doesn't sound right.

B: Wait a minute. How do you know the singer is in love?

A: It's supposed to be a love song.

B: But I don't like the way "love" sounds.

C: Neither do I.

A: Why not?

B: It's too obvious.

A: That's true. Well, what do you think about "need"?
    "I will always need you."

B: Not great, but not bad.

C: So let's choose "need."

A: OK . . . for now—maybe we'll change it later.

C: So what about line 2?

Decide and Write

With other members of your group, choose the best words for each song.

Song 1: A Love Song for Whitney Houston
(For this song, circle the word from each group you think is best.)

1. I will always   like   you.
                    love
                    remember
                    need

2. Every time I   touch   you, I feel   sad   inside.
                  kiss   warm
                  see   bad
                  hug   good

3. You are my   heart.
                 soul
                 man
                 love

4. Last night I   loved   you with another   woman.
                 saw   love
                 imagined   lover
                 found   feeling

5. It made me feel so   good.
                       bad
                       jealous
                       angry

6. I thought I was going to   fly.
                              cry
                              die
                              lie

7. I will never   love   you.
                 like
                 kiss
                 leave

8. Every time I   touch   you, I feel   bad   inside.
                      kiss   warm
                      see   sad
                      hug   good

9. You are my   heart.
                   soul
                   man
                   love

10. This morning I called   my mother   on the phone.
                            my friend
                            your sister
                            your lover

11. She told me to   forget   you.
                    marry
                    talk to
                    kill

12. I said I   would.
            couldn't
            should
            might

13. But when I came into your   house,   you were   so sweet.
                              apartment   sick
                              room   alone
                              arms   gone

14. How will   you   know if   you   really   love(s)   you?
               she   I   like(s)   me
               I   we   hate(s)   her
               we   she   want(s)   us

15. Will   I   ever really   find   you?
           you   love   her
           she   leave   me
           we   marry   each other

16. I just can't   eat   without you.
                  get married
                  live
                  love

17. My heart is   in love.
                  like a flower
                  breaking
                  yours

18. I will always   need   you.
                  love
                  remember
                  hate

19. Every time I   touch you, I feel   sick.
                  see   warm
                  kiss   good
                  think of   sad

20. You are   my heart.
           my soul
           my lover
           nothing to me

Song 2: A Rock Song for Guns N' Roses
(For this song, fill in the blanks with whatever words you want.)

1. I took a ride _____.

2. I saw a _____.

3. I didn't _____.

4. What _____?

5. What _____?

6. What _____?

7. I ate a _____.

8. I killed a _____.

9. I didn't _____.

10. Where _____?

11. When _____?

12. How much _____?

13. I ran _____.

14. I loved _____.

15. I didn't _____.

16. Why _____?

17. Why _____?

18. Why _____?

19. I never _____.

20. I never _____.

Song 3: A Rock or Love Song for Legs
(For this song, write whatever words you want.)

1. _____

2. _____

3. _____

4. _____

5. _____

6. _____

7. _____

8. _____

9. _____

10. _____

11. _____

12. _____

13. _____

14. _____

15. _____

16. _____

17. _____

18. _____

19. _____

20. _____

Discuss

Share your songs with another group. Look at the other group's songs carefully. Do they sound good? Do they make sense? Tell the other group what you like and what you don't like.

Extend

Written/Oral Assignment

1. Choose your group's best song. Think of some music to go with it. Practice it with your group and sing it to the class.

kiss   slap

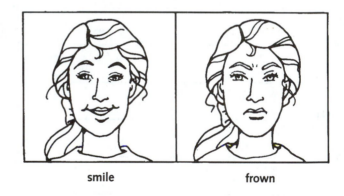

smile   frown

strong   weak

warm   cool

Cultural Contact Assignment

2. Choose a singer (or musical group) that you like. Go to a record store. Find some of the singer's (or group's) CDs and cassettes. Then fill in the blanks below. Discuss your information with your class.

Name of singer (or group): _____

CDs in store: _____

_____

_____

_____

_____

Cassettes in store: _____

_____

_____

_____

_____

_____

How Will You Plan Your Family's Budget?

Vocabulary

a place   a place to live in

income   money

maintenance   taking care of

pregnant   about to have a baby

collision   protecting cars

coverage   included

charities   groups that give free food and clothes

liability   protecting people

mild   not too cold

appliances   electrical machines

Read and Consider

You are a family in Oklahoma City, Oklahoma. Your family includes a wife (age 24), a husband (25), the wife's mother (63), and the husband and wife's daughter (2). You came to the United States six months ago. Until now, you have been living with friends, but you need to find a place of your own.

Your income is very small, about $1500 a month. The wife is a book translator, and the husband is washing dishes in a restaurant. The wife's mother stays at home and baby-sits for the daughter. Yesterday, the wife went to a doctor and found out she is pregnant.

You must plan your budget before you can move.

Decide and Write

Before talking with your family, write down your choices. Write down a reason for each choice.

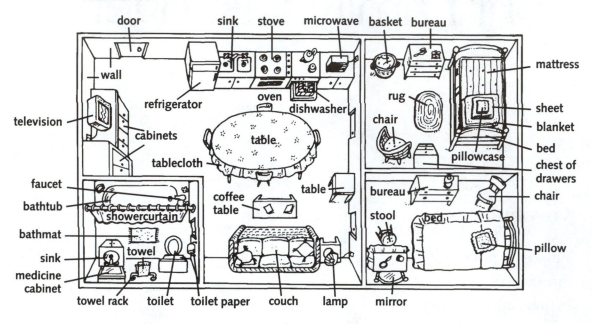

Area 1: **Housing**
You must find an apartment of your own. Your choices are:
  A. A studio apartment (3 rooms: a kitchen, a living room/bedroom, and a bathroom. $325 a month.)
  B. A one-bedroom apartment (3 rooms: a kitchen/living room, a bathroom, and a bedroom. $475 a month.)
  C. A two-bedroom apartment (4 rooms: a kitchen/living room, a bathroom, and two bedrooms. $600 a month.)

  Your choice and why: _____

  _____

Area 2: **Food**
Before now, you spent about $75 a week for food. But now the daughter is getting bigger, and a new baby will come soon. Your choices are:
  A. Decrease the amount for food to $250 a month.
  B. Spend the same as before: $300 a month.
  C. Increase the amount for food to $350 a month.

  Your choice and why: _____

  _____

Area 3: **Medical Insurance**

Before now, only the wife has had insurance. The cost is $170 a month. But the daughter has been sick a lot, and a new baby will come soon.

Your choices are:

A. Continue to insure only the wife: $170 a month.

B. Insure the wife, the daughter, and the new baby (when it comes): $275 a month.

C. Insure all of the family: $375 a month.

Your choice and why: _____

_____

Area 4: **Electricity**

You have no choice about electricity. The average cost is $75 a month.

Area 5: **Telephone**

Your choices are:

A. No telephone.

B. A telephone (basic service $25 a month).

Your choice and why: _____

_____

Area 6: **Car Maintenance and Gas**

You do not have any choice. The husband must have a car to get to work. The cost of maintaining your old car is about $50 a month. The cost of gas is about $60 a month. So, your total cost is $110 a month.

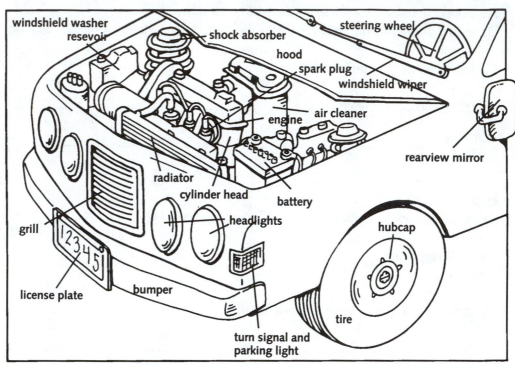

Area 7: **Car Insurance**

The state of Oklahoma requires all drivers to have car insurance. The choices are:

A. Liability insurance: $79 a month.

B. Liability and collision insurance: $199 a month.

C. No insurance (illegal).

Your choice and why: _____

_____

SKELTON-MORRIS ASSOCIATES

P.O. BOX 130
HARTWELL, GA 30643
(404) 376-8035

NAME & ADDRESS:

_____

_____

_____

AUTOMOBILE QUOTE

DATE _____

PHONE NUMBER WORK _____ HOME _____

PRESENT CARRIER _____

EXPIRATION DATE _____

REASON FOR CHANGE (CANCELLED, NON-RENEWED, PRICE)

_____

DO YOU OWN A HOME? _____

Full Name of All Drivers	License Number/State/Social Security Number	Date of Birth Mo./Day/Yr.	Sex	Marital Status	Drivers Training	**At School
A.						
B.						
C.						
D.						
E.						

**OVER 100 MI. W/O CAR

Car	Year	Make / Model / Body Style	Estimated Annual Mileage	Is Car Driven to Work/School Yes	No	Mileage One Way	Farm Use? Yes	No	Business Use? Yes	No
1.				☐	☐		☐	☐	☐	☐
2.				☐	☐		☐	☐	☐	☐
3.				☐	☐		☐	☐	☐	☐
4.				☐	☐		☐	☐	☐	☐

Car	Who Drives What Car	Occupation	Employer	Currently a Good Student (Must Have "B" Average)
1.				
2.				
3.				
4.				

List any accidents or violations which have occurred in the last THREE years.

Operator	Date	Where	Description (If violation, give date of conviction)	Any Property Damage? ($)	Any Bodily Injury? ($)

The Sun, Hartwell, GA

Area 8: **Clothing**

Winter is coming and you need warm clothes (Oklahoma has cold winters). Your choices are:

A. Buy no clothes; get free clothes from charities.
B. Spend $50 a month.
C. Spend $100 a month.

Your choice and why: _____

_____

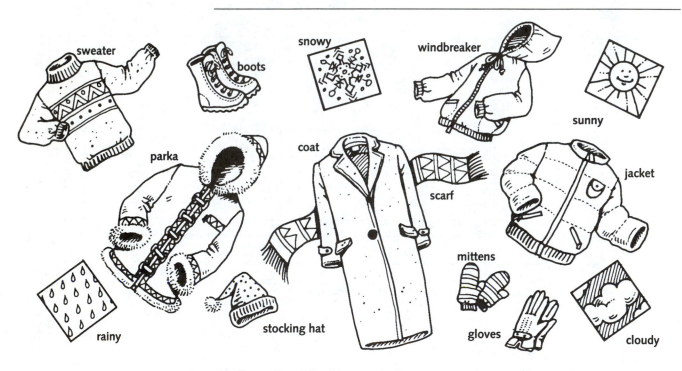

sweater   boots   snowy   windbreaker   sunny

parka   coat   scarf   jacket

rainy   stocking hat   mittens   gloves   cloudy

Area 9: **Spending Money**

You would like to go to a movie once a month. Also, it would be nice to eat at a restaurant sometimes. Your choices are:

A. Never go out.
B. Go to one movie a month: $25 a month.
C. Go to one movie and one restaurant a month: $50 a month.

Your choice and why: _____

_____

Area 10: **Emergency Savings**
You want to save money for the future. Your choices are:
A. Save nothing.
B. Save $50 a month.
C. Save $100 a month.
    Your choice and why: _____

_____

Area 11: **Appliance Money**
You do not have a choice. You will rent a TV, refrigerator, stove, and washing machine for $195 a month.

Summary of Expenses

	For what	*How much*
1.	_____	_____
2.	_____	_____
3.	_____	_____
4.	_____	_____
5.	_____	_____
6.	_____	_____
7.	_____	_____
8.	_____	_____
9.	_____	_____
10.	_____	_____
11.	_____	_____
	Total:	_____
		(must be $1500 or less)

Prediscussion

In this discussion, you will be talking to your family. Your discussion will be very informal. You will either agree or disagree with your family.

Also, you will be making suggestions. Study the following expressions. Repeat each one after your teacher, then practice them with a partner. Fill in the blanks [. . .] with your own words. Take turns making suggestions, agreeing, and disagreeing.

Making Suggestions

I definitely think that we should . . .
We should . . .
I think that we should . . .
I suggest that we . . .
I believe that we ought to . . .
I think that maybe we should . . .

Agreeing

Great idea.
Definitely.

I agree.
Good idea.
Me too.
So do I.
I do too.
I think so too.
That sounds good.
Sounds good to me.
That makes sense.

That seems like a good idea.
I guess that's a good idea.
Maybe so.

Disagreeing

You've got to be kidding.*
No way.*

I disagree.
I don't think that's a good idea.
That doesn't make sense.
I don't think so.

I'm not sure that's a good idea.
That sounds good, but . . .

*Remember that these expressions may be considered impolite.

Continue practicing the expressions with two partners. Begin with the examples.

Example 1   A: I think that we should spend $100 a month for clothes.
              B: I guess that's a good idea.
              C: I don't think so.
              B: Why not?

Example 2   C: I believe that we ought to rent a studio apartment.
              B: I really disagree with that!
              A: I don't. It seems like a good idea to me.
              B: Why?

Study the following discussion. See how the expressions are used. Practice the discussion with your two classmates. Take turns being A, B, and C (A = grandmother, B = wife, C = husband).

A: Why don't we rent the studio apartment?
B: I don't think that's a good idea because it's too small.
C: But it's cheap.
B: That sounds good, but how will all of us live in a studio apartment?
A: So what do you suggest?
B: The two-bedroom apartment.
C: That doesn't make sense.
A: Why not?
C: It's $600 a month.
B: All you think about is money.
C: Come on, give me a break. Our total income is only $1500 a month. Of course I worry about money.
B: You think you're the only one worrying about money?
A: Why don't we compromise? How about the one-bedroom apartment?
B: Too small.
C: Too expensive.
A: You know . . . let's come back to housing later.
B: Well . . . I guess that's a good idea.
C: Maybe so.

Discuss

For this discussion, your group should have at least three people. Each person should pretend to be a family member: one grandmother, one wife, and one husband. After you reach a decision about the budget, exchange family roles and have the discussion one more time.

Extend

Written/Oral Assignment

1. Write a budget of your monthly expenses now. Do **not** include the actual amount of money you spend. Instead, write down the percentage (%) of your total budget for each area. Afterward, write down a typical budget for you in your native city. What similarities and differences are there? Discuss your observations with your class.

	Here	*Native City*		*Here*	*Native City*
Housing:	____	____	Clothing:	____	____
Food:	____	____	Electricity:	____	____
Insurance:	____	____	Entertainment:	____	____
Telephone:	____	____	Educational Expense:	____	____
Transportation:	____	____	Savings:	____	____
Other:	____	____			

Cultural Contact Assignment

2. Bring a newspaper to class. Look at the classified ads and check the cost of apartments. Choose one advertisement. Think of three questions to ask a person about the apartment. With a classmate, write a telephone conversation and role-play it.

    If possible call the number in the ad. Discuss your telephone conversation with the class.

Hair, Hair! What's the Sweetest Hair?

Vocabulary

fanciest   most decorated

on top   the best

"sweet"   "cool," good

as well as   in addition to

clients   customers

evaluate   to check

"history"   finished, out of style

Read and Consider

Hair styles change all the time. One hair style becomes popular; another hair style becomes unpopular. Your group owns the fanciest, most popular, most expensive hair salon in Los Angeles, Hairway to the Stars.

Your clients include all the famous movie and TV actresses and actors—as well as some students and working people.

Every week, you evaluate the twelve most popular hair styles for women and men. You keep eight and throw out four. To replace the four you throw out, you design four new styles. This is how your hair salon stays on top. Today is evaluation day.

Decide and Write

Before talking with your group, evaluate the styles. Do not design the new hair styles until you talk with your group.

    Remember, you must throw out four for women and four for men.

    The evaluation code is

        10   looks great! sweet! "in"
         7   looks good
         5   looks so-so, not special
         3   looks bad, kind of old
         0   YUK! History!

For Women:

1   2   3

Code #: _____   Code #: _____   Code #: _____

4   5   6

Code #: _____   Code #: _____   Code #: _____

7   8   9

Code #: _____   Code #: _____   Code #: _____

Code #: _____

Code #: _____

Code #: _____

Which women's style do you like the best? _____   Why? _____

_____

Which women's styles will you throw out? _____ , _____ , _____ , _____ .

Make four new styles for women:

For Men:

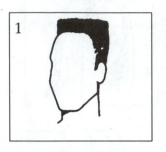

Code #: _____

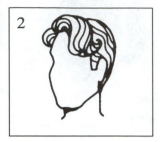

Code #: _____

Code #: _____

Code #: _____

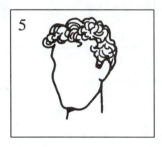

Code #: _____

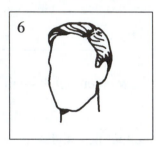

Code #: _____

Code #: _____

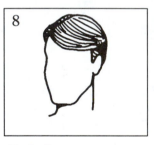

Code #: _____

Code #: _____

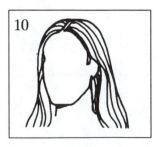

Code #: _____

Code #: _____

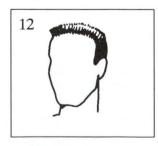

Code #: _____

Which men's style do you like the best? _____   Why? _____

_____

Which four men's styles will you throw out? _____ , _____ , _____ , _____ .

Make four new styles for men:

1	2

3	4

Prediscussion

In this discussion, you will be talking about popular hair styles. Your language will include slang. Study the following conversation expressions. Repeat each one after your teacher. Then practice them with two partners. Take turns describing a style, agreeing, and disagreeing.

Describing a Style	*Agreeing*	*Disagreeing*
That looks great/hot!	You're right about that.	Come on, give me a break.*
That looks good.	I think so too.	You've got to be kidding.*
Looks good to me.	To me too.	Not to me.
I like the way that looks.	So do I.	No way.*
I think that looks pretty good.	I do too.	I don't (think so).
It's OK.	I guess so.	You really think so?
I think that looks pretty bad.	Me too.	I don't (think so).
I don't like the way that looks.	Me either.	I do.
Looks strange to me.	To me too.	Not to me.
That doesn't look good.	I don't think so either.	I think it does.
That's history!	Definitely.	You've got to be kidding.
That's awful.	You can say that again.	No way.

Continue practicing the expressions with your two partners. Begin with the examples.

Example 1   A: Curly hair is really hot!
B: You're right about that.
C: No way.

Example 2   A: I think straight hair looks pretty bad.
B: Me too.
C: I don't.

*Remember these expressions may be considered impolite.

Study the following conversation. See how the expressions are used. Practice the conversation with a partner.

A: How do you like long curly hair?
B: OK, but short wavy hair is better.
A: You really think so? I think it looks pretty bad.
B: I don't think so. It's hot.
A: No way. Long curly hair is in. Short wavy hair is history.
B: You've got that backwards. Anyway, what do you think about long straight hair on men?
A: Truth?
B: Yeah. What do you think?
A: Looks strange to me. What about you?
B: I kind of like it.
A: You've got to be kidding.
B: No, really, it looks pretty good.
A: Well, if you say so.*

Discuss

Talk with your group. Explain your opinions. Agree on what's "in" and what's "out."

Draw designs of the new hairstyles with your group. Afterwards, share your designs with the class. Choose the best designs in the class.

Extend

Written/Oral Assignment

1. With a partner, write a conversation between a hairdresser and an unhappy customer. The customer is unhappy because the hairdresser did not cut the customer's hair well. After you write the conversation, give your conversation to another group (they will give their conversation to you). Read and discuss both conversations with the other group. Make corrections if necessary. Role-play the other group's conversation for the class.

Cultural Contact Assignment

2. Visit a hair salon or barber shop. Look carefully at all of the features of the salon or shop. Discuss your observations with your class.

*This does not mean that A necessarily agrees with B. It means that A is willing to accept B's opinion.

What's the Right Thing to Do?

Vocabulary

vegetarian   a person who doesn't eat meat

roasted   cooked

stuffed   full

toast   a good luck wish before drinking

common sense   good judgment

Read and Consider

Manners change as well as hair styles. What was polite in 1990 may not be polite in the year 2000. It is time to write a new book, *Manners 2000*.

   Your group is writing the chapter "A Guest at Dinner." You should use your experience, education, and common sense to help you. You must think about good and bad manners.

Decide and Write

Before talking with your co-writers, circle the letter of the most polite choice. Write down a reason for each choice.

Situation 1: You are invited to dinner at a person's house. You should:

A. Take a bottle of wine with you.
B. Bring a salad.
C. Take some flowers and candy.
D. Take nothing.
E. (Other)

Reason for choice: _____

_____

Situation 2: You are invited for dinner at 7:00 P.M. You should:

A. Arrive at 6:30.
B. Arrive at 6:45.
C. Arrive at 7:05.
D. Arrive between 7:00 and 7:30.
E. (Other)

Reason for choice: _____

_____

Situation 3: You are the only guest. Everyone sits down to eat. The food is on the table. You should:

A. Serve yourself and begin to eat.
B. Wait for your host or hostess to serve you.
C. Serve yourself, but wait for your host or hostess to eat first.
D. Serve your host and hostess.
E. (Other)

Reason for choice: _____

_____

Situation 4: You sit down to eat, but the food looks very strange. The roasted chicken looks like dog meat, and the broccoli looks like grass. You should:

A. Politely refuse to eat.
B. Pretend you are sick.
C. Eat a couple of bites and say you're on a diet.
D. Eat normally.
E. (Other)

Reason for choice: _____

_____

Situation 5: You sit down to eat. You are a vegetarian, but all the food is either meat or cooked with meat. You should:

A. Politely refuse to eat.
B. Pretend you are sick.
C. Eat a couple of bites and say you're on a diet.
D. Eat normally.
E. (Other)

Reason for choice: _____

_____

Situation 6: Everyone sits down to eat. The host says, "Please hold hands, close your eyes, and repeat this religious blessing after me." You are not religious. You should:

A. Explain to everyone that you are not religious.
B. Say nothing and do the same as everyone else.
C. Hold hands and close eyes but do not repeat the blessing.
D. Ask to leave the table for a minute.
E. (Other)

Reason for choice: _____

_____

Situation 7: Everyone sits down to eat. Before you start, the host pours something in everyone's glasses and makes a toast. You realize that it is wine, but you never drink alcohol. You should:

A. Pretend to drink a little.
B. Say that you never drink alcohol.
C. Ask for a glass of water.
D. Say nothing and don't drink.
E. (Other)

Reason for choice: _____

_____

Situation 8: You sit down to eat. You are extremely hungry! You take one bite, and YUK! It is the worst food you have ever eaten. You should:

A. Get up and leave.
B. Play with your food and pretend to eat some.
C. Tell the host and hostess how good the food is.
D. Tell the host and hostess something is wrong with your food.
E. (Other)

Reason for choice: _____

_____

Situation 9: You are eating dinner. The food is good, but you've been feeling bad all day. Suddenly, your stomach feels like it will explode. You should:

A. Run to the bathroom.
B. Ask to leave the table.
C. Try to control the pain.
D. Drink a lot of water.
E. (Other)

Reason for choice: _____

_____

Situation 10: The dinner is almost over. The food was great and you are stuffed. You turn around to talk to the person beside you, and your hostess puts more food on your plate. You should:

A. Put some of the food onto the plate of the person beside you.
B. Eat a little more and say you're full.
C. Try to eat all the food.
D. Politely refuse to eat.
E. (Other)

Reason for choice: _____

_____

Situation 11: The meal is over. The food was great. You should:

A. Ask who cooked the food and thank her or him.
B. Burp loudly.
C. Thank both your host and hostess.
D. Stand up and clap your hands loudly.
E. (Other)

Reason for choice: _____

_____

Situation 12: The meal is over, and all of the dirty dishes are on the table. You should:

A. Move to another room.
B. Ask if you can help clean the table.
C. Light a cigarette.
D. Take your plate and glass to the kitchen.
E. (Other)

Reason for choice: _____

_____

Situation 13: It has been a wonderful evening. It's 11:30 P.M. and you're tired. Your host and hostess continue to talk. You should:

A. Ask them what time they usually go to bed.
B. Lie down on the sofa.
C. Yawn a lot.
D. Wait for your host or hostess to say it's time for you to go.
E. (Other)

Reason for choice: _____

_____

Prediscussion

In this discussion, you will be talking to your co-writers. Your discussion will be about manners. You will decide what is polite and what is impolite.

Study the following conversation expressions. Repeat each one after your teacher. Then practice them with two partners. Fill in the blanks [. . .] with your own words. Take turns giving an idea, agreeing, and disagreeing.

Giving an Idea	Agreeing	Disagreeing
I think that a guest should . . .	So do I.	I don't (think so).
I think that it is polite to . . .	I think so too.	I don't (think so).
I think that it is OK to . . .	Me too.	I don't (think so).
I think that it is all right to . . .	I do too.	I don't (think so).
I don't think that a guest should . . .	I don't think so either.	I think it's all right.
I don't think that it's polite to . . .	Me either.	I think it's OK.

Continue practicing the expressions with your two partners. Begin with the examples.

Example 1   A: I think that a guest should burp loudly.
              B: So do I.
              C: Me too.

Example 2   C: I don't think that it's polite to yawn a lot.
              B: Me either.
              A: I think it's OK.

Study the following discussion. See how the expressions are used. Practice the discussion with your two classmates.

A: I don't think that a guest should take anything to a person's house.
B: Me either.
C: Why not?
B: Because in my country it's impolite for a guest to take something to a person's house.
A: In my country too.
C: Well, in my country, a guest should take some flowers or candy to a person's house.
B: Oh really?
C: Don't you think it's OK to do that?
A: It's OK in your country, but not in my country.
C: That's true, but *Manners 2000* is not just for your country.
A: Or just for your country.
B: So, what's the best choice?
C: Maybe E. We should think of a new choice.
A: Good idea.

Discuss

Talk with your co-writers. Explain your opinions. Agree on the most polite behavior.

Write down five important things for a guest to say or do, and five things a guest should **never** say or do. Share your ideas with the class.

Write down five important things for a guest to say or do.

1. _____

2. _____

3. _____

4. _____

5. _____

Write down five things a guest should **never** say or do.

1. _____

2. _____

3. _____

4. _____

5. _____

Extend

Written/Oral Assignment

1. Write a paragraph about guest and table customs of people in your country. Include as many different customs as you can. Share your paragraph with your class.

Cultural Contact Assignment

2. To prepare yourself for formal dinner situations in the United States, bring plates, glasses, silverware, and napkins to class for formal dinner practice.

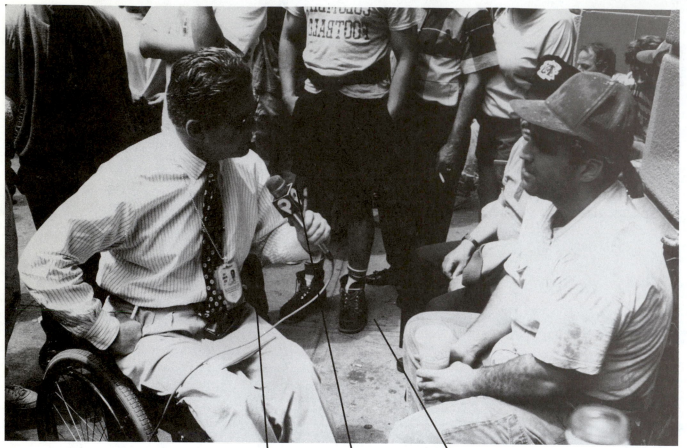

presscard   microphone   sidewalk

Playing Favorites

Vocabulary

article   story

co-workers   people you work with

relative   family member

spare time   free time

aside from   not including

Read and Consider

You work for the "People" department of the Minneapolis, Minnesota newspaper, *The Times*. Once a year, the People department goes into the streets of Minneapolis and asks questions. These questions are about many different subjects.

This year, your department is going to ask people about their favorite things. Specifically, you are going to ask the 20 questions that follow. After you get the answers, you will write a newspaper article about the answers.

Before going out into the street, you need to practice asking the questions to your co-workers.

Preconversation

In this conversation, you will:

1. Introduce yourself.

2. Ask for permission to ask a few questions.

3. Ask three questions from the list.

4. Show interest and ask follow-up questions if you want to.

5. Pre-close the conversation.

6. Close the conversation.

In this interview conversation, you will be talking to a stranger. Your language will be formal. Study the following conversation expressions. Repeat them after your teacher. Then practice them with a partner. Fill in the blanks [. . .] with your name. Take turns introducing yourself and responding.

Introducing Yourself and Asking for Permission

Possible Responses

Excuse me, my name is . . . and I work for the *Minneapolis Times* newspaper. May I ask you a few questions?

Sure, go ahead.
It's fine. I don't mind at all.
Sorry, but I don't have time
   right now.

Excuse me, my name is . . . and I work for the *Minneapolis Times* newspaper. Would you mind if I asked you a few questions?

Not today.
What for?
What kinds of questions?

Pre-Closing the Conversation If the Person Answers the Questions.

Thank you very much for your time.
Thank you very much.

My pleasure.
You're welcome. No problem.

Pre-Closing the Conversation If the Person Doesn't Answer.

Well, thanks anyway.

OK.

Study the following conversations. See how the expressions are used. Practice the conversations with your partner.

Conversation 1

A: Excuse me, my name is . . . and I work for the *Minneapolis Times* newspaper. May I ask you a few questions?
B: Sorry, but I don't have time right now.
A: Well, thanks anyway.
B: OK.

Conversation 2

A: Excuse me, my name is . . . and I work for the *Minneapolis Times* newspaper. Would you mind if I asked you a few questions?
B: What for?
A: For a special edition of our newspaper.
B: Sure, go ahead.
A: These questions are about your favorite things. First of all, what is your favorite food?
B: Let's see. My favorite kind of food is Mexican food. I like burritos the best.
A: OK. Second, what is your favorite season?
B: That's easy. Summer.
A: All right. And last—what's your favorite book?
B: That's a tough one. Let me think a minute. I would say [name of book] . . . by [author] . . . .
A: OK. That's all the questions I have. Thank you very much for your time.
B: You're welcome.
A: Good-bye.
B: Bye.

Decide and Write

Stand up and walk around the room. Ask three questions to each person. Try to talk to all of your classmates at least two times. Listen carefully and write down their answers. Pretend that you are talking to strangers.

1. What's your favorite food?

    Person 1: _____

    Person 2: _____

    Person 3: _____

    Person 4: _____

    Person 5: _____

2. What's your favorite movie?

    Person 1: _____

    Person 2: _____

    Person 3: _____

    Person 4: _____

    Person 5: _____

3. What's your favorite color?

    Person 1: _____

    Person 2: _____

    Person 3: _____

    Person 4: _____

    Person 5: _____

4. What's your favorite season?

   Person 1: _____

   Person 2: _____

   Person 3: _____

   Person 4: _____

   Person 5: _____

5. What's your favorite animal?

   Person 1: _____

   Person 2: _____

   Person 3: _____

   Person 4: _____

   Person 5: _____

6. Who's your favorite relative?

   Person 1: _____

   Person 2: _____

   Person 3: _____

   Person 4: _____

   Person 5: _____

7. What's your favorite book?

    Person 1: _____

    Person 2: _____

    Person 3: _____

    Person 4: _____

    Person 5: _____

8. What's your favorite sport?

    Person 1: _____

    Person 2: _____

    Person 3: _____

    Person 4: _____

    Person 5: _____

9. Who's your favorite actor?

    Person 1: _____

    Person 2: _____

    Person 3: _____

    Person 4: _____

    Person 5: _____

10. Who's your favorite actress?

   Person 1: _____

   Person 2: _____

   Person 3: _____

   Person 4: _____

   Person 5: _____

11. What's your favorite thing to do in your spare time?

   Person 1: _____

   Person 2: _____

   Person 3: _____

   Person 4: _____

   Person 5: _____

12. When you were a child, what was your favorite toy?

   Person 1: _____

   Person 2: _____

   Person 3: _____

   Person 4: _____

   Person 5: _____

13. Who's your favorite singer?

    Person 1: _____

    Person 2: _____

    Person 3: _____

    Person 4: _____

    Person 5: _____

14. What's your favorite drink?

    Person 1: _____

    Person 2: _____

    Person 3: _____

    Person 4: _____

    Person 5: _____

15. What's your favorite joke?

    Person 1: _____

    Person 2: _____

    Person 3: _____

    Person 4: _____

    Person 5: _____

16. What's your favorite magazine?

Person 1: _____

Person 2: _____

Person 3: _____

Person 4: _____

Person 5: _____

17. Who's your favorite cartoon character?

Person 1: _____

Person 2: _____

Person 3: _____

Person 4: _____

Person 5: _____

18. What's your favorite car?

Person 1: _____

Person 2: _____

Person 3: _____

Person 4: _____

Person 5: _____

19. What's your favorite time of day?

   Person 1: _____

   Person 2: _____

   Person 3: _____

   Person 4: _____

   Person 5: _____

20. Aside from your native country, what is your favorite country in the world?

   Person 1: _____

   Person 2: _____

   Person 3: _____

   Person 4: _____

   Person 5: _____

Discuss

When you finish asking questions to the class, discuss the answers as a group. Were there any similar answers? Did everyone have different answers?

Extend

Written/Oral Assignment

1. Write a letter to your best friend. Tell your friend about your favorite things to do and favorite places to go to in the city you are in now.

Cultural Contact Assignment

2. Choose five of the questions from the list of 20 in this unit. Ask these questions to at least three Americans. Write down their answers carefully and report on your results to the class.

Where Do You Want to Go?

Vocabulary

agency   company
reasonably   moderately
breaks   vacations
assigned   given

Read and Consider

You are travel agents in a travel agency in Salt Lake City, Utah. Salt Lake City is in a beautiful location. Hundreds of international students come to you for travel information.

The manager of your office wants you to plan a student tour. More specifically:

1. The tour should begin in Salt Lake City and end in Salt Lake City.

2. The tour should use buses for transportation.

3. The tour should last 12 days.

4. The tour should not cost too much.

Prediscussion

Look briefly at Day 1 in the *Decide and Write* section. In this discussion, you will be talking about places for international students to go. Study the following conversation expressions. Practice them with your teacher. Fill in the blanks [. . .] with your own words.

Giving an Opinion

I think that they would/might like to go to . . .
I think that it would/might be interesting for them to see . . .
I think that they should spend the night in . . .

I don't think that they would like to go to . . .
I don't think that it would be interesting for them to see . . .
I don't think that they should spend the night in . . .

People in small discussion groups are often shy about giving their opinions. The following expressions can be used to ask a person about his or her opinion. Practice using them with your teacher.

Asking for an Opinion from Your Classmate

Well, what do you think?
What's your opinion?
How do you feel about that?
Don't you agree?
Do you think that's a good idea?
You know what I mean?
Tell me what you think.

Continue practicing the expressions with two partners. Begin with the examples.

Example 1   A: I think that they might like to go to Yellowstone National Park.
B: —
C: —
A: Well, what do you think?
B: That's a great idea!
C: I think so too.

Example 2   B: I don't think it would be interesting for them to see Nevada.
                A: —
                C: —
                B: Well, how do you feel about that?
                A: I don't think so either.
                C: I disagree. Reno and Las Vegas are great places to visit.

Study the following discussion. See how the expressions are used. Practice the discussion with three of your classmates.

A: OK. They are starting in Salt Lake City. Do you think they should go north toward Yellowstone or south toward the Grand Canyon?
D: Why not west toward San Francisco or east toward Denver?
C: San Francisco is too far.
D: It's only two days by bus. They have 12 days.
B: I think that most international students would rather see the Grand Canyon anyway.
A: Me too.
C: I'm not so sure. But at least they can go south first. OK?
D: It's OK with me.
A: So they will leave Salt Lake City on Highway 15. Where will they stop first?
D: I think that they'd like to go to Zion National Park.
B: Sounds good to me.
C: Zion National Park? What can you do there?
B: Well . . . not much, but it is beautiful.
A: And cheap.
C: OK. What else can they see around Zion?
D: What about Bryce Canyon?
C: I don't think that they'd like to go there.
B: Neither do I.
A: Me either. So what else can they see?

Decide and Write

Talk with your fellow travel agents. Look at the maps and other information. Explain your opinions carefully. Write down your choices.

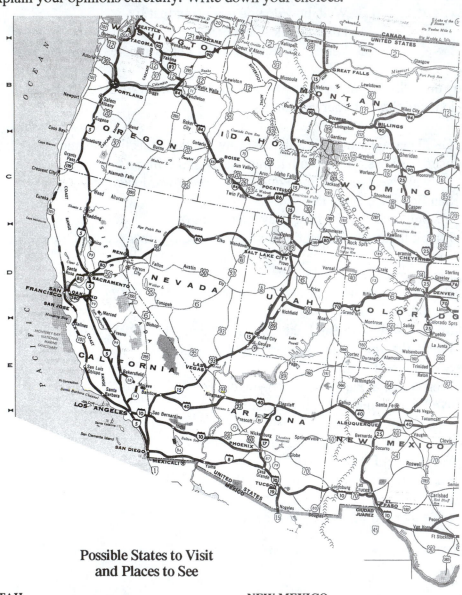

**Possible States to Visit
and Places to See**

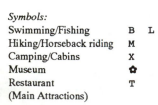

Symbols:

Swimming/Fishing	B L
Hiking/Horseback riding	M
Camping/Cabins	X
Museum	✿
Restaurant	T
(Main Attractions)	

UTAH

Great Salt Lake M B L X T
   (Unusal water)
Bryce Canyon Park M X
   (Beautiful landscape)
Zion National Park M ✿ T X

COLORADO

Dinosaur National Monument M B L ✿ X
   (Dinosaur bones)
Rocky Mountains Naitonal Park M ✿ X

NEW MEXICO

Santa Fe
   (Native American
   and Spanish history)
Carlsbad Caverns National Park M ✿ T
   (Deep underground caverns)
White Sands Naitonal Monument M ✿
   (Beautiful desert)

ARIZONA

Grand Canyon National Park   M   B L   ✿   T
  (Unusual landscape)
Petrified Forest National Park   M   ✿   T
  (Unusual Rocks)
Saguaro National Monument   M   ✿

NEVADA

Las Vegas
  (Casinos)
Reno
  (Casinos)
Hoover Dam   B L
  (Highest dam in U.S.)

CALIFORNIA

San Francisco
  (Golden Gate Bridge, Chinatown, cablecars)
Los Angeles
  (Disneyland, Beverly Hills)
San Diego
  (San Diego Zoo)
Redwood National Park   M   B L X   ✿
  (Tall trees)
Yosemite National Park   M   B L X   ✿   T
  (Beautiful landscape)
Death Valley National
  Monument   M   X   ✿   T
  (Desert)
Joshua Tree National Monument   M   ✿   X
  (Beautiful landscape)

WYOMING

Continental Divide   M
  (Mountains)
Yellowstone National Park   M   B L X   ✿   T
  (Unusual animals, geysers, beauty)

MONTANA

Glacier National Park   M   B L X   ✿   T
  (Glaciers, bears)
Grand Teton National Park   M   B L X   ✿   T
  (Mountains)

IDAHO

Sun Valley
  (Skiiing)
Craters of the Moon National Park   M   X   ✿
  (Unusual landscape)

WASHINGTON

Seattle
  (Space needle, beauty)
Cascades National Park   B L M
  (Mountains)

OREGON

Crater Lake National Park   M   B L X   ✿   T
  (Beautiful landscape)

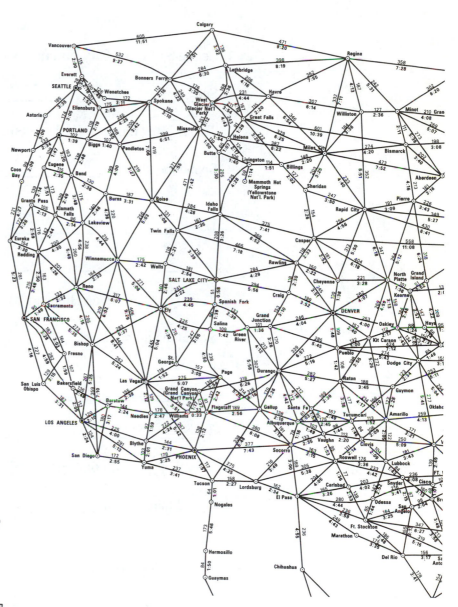

Transcontinental
Mileage and Driving Time Map

Explanation

227   Light numerals indicate mileage in statue miles.

7:55   **Bold** numerals indicate driving time.

Driving time shown is approximate under normal conditions. Consideration has been given to topography, number of towns along route, congested urban areas, and the federally imposed maximum 55 m.p.h. speed law.

Allowances should be made for night driving and unusually fast or slow drivers.

Day 1: Leave Salt Lake City on Highway _____ .

See _____, _____ , _____ .

Travel _____ miles on Highway(s) _____, _____, _____ .

Spend the night in _____ .

Day 2: Leave _____ on Highway _____ .

See _____, _____ , _____ .

Travel _____ miles on Highway(s) _____, _____, _____ .

Spend the night in _____ .

Day 3: Leave _____ on Highway _____ .

See _____, _____ , _____ .

Travel _____ miles on Highway(s) _____, _____, _____ .

Spend the night in _____ .

Day 4: Leave _____ on Highway _____ .

See _____, _____ , _____ .

Travel _____ miles on Highway(s) _____, _____, _____ .

Spend the night in _____ .

Day 5: Leave _____ on Highway _____ .

   See _____ , _____ , _____ .

   Travel ____ miles on Highway(s) _____ , _____ , _____ .

   Spend the night in _____ .

Day 6: Leave _____ on Highway _____ .

   See _____ , _____ , _____ .

   Travel ____ miles on Highway(s) _____ , _____ , _____ .

   Spend the night in _____ .

Day 7: Leave _____ on Highway _____ .

   See _____ , _____ , _____ .

   Travel ____ miles on Highway(s) _____ , _____ , _____ .

   Spend the night in _____ .

Day 8: Leave _____ on Highway _____ .

   See _____ , _____ , _____ .

   Travel ____ miles on Highway(s) _____ , _____ , _____ .

   Spend the night in _____ .

Day 9: Leave _____ on Highway _____ .

   See _____ , _____ , _____ .

   Travel ____ miles on Highway(s) _____ , _____ , _____ .

   Spend the night in _____ .

Day 10: Leave _____ on Highway _____ .

See _____ , _____ , _____ .

Travel ____ miles on Highway(s) _____ , _____ , _____ .

Spend the night in _____ .

Day 11: Leave _____ on Highway _____ .

See _____ , _____ , _____ .

Travel ____ miles on Highway(s) _____ , _____ , _____ .

Spend the night in _____ .

Day 12: Leave _____ on Highway _____ .

See _____ , _____ , _____ .

Travel ____ miles on Highway(s) _____ , _____ , _____ .

Spend the night in _____*Salt Lake City*_____ .

Trip Summary

Miles Traveled: _____

Cost: _____

Discuss

After planning the trip with your fellow travel agents, discuss your plan with the rest of the class. Which group has the best plan?

Extend

Written/Oral Assignment

1. Design a tour of your native country (or, if there are many people from your country in your class, your native city). Choose at least ten good places for a tourist to visit. Present your tour to your class.

Cultural Contact Assignment

2. Go to a travel agency. Pick up some brochures about a travel destination in your area. Share your findings with the class.

What's on the Ice Cream Menu?

Vocabulary

humidity   water in the air

sundae   big bowl of ice cream with topping

marvelous   wonderful

bet   to think

Read and Consider

It's summertime in Charleston, South Carolina. The temperature is hot, and the humidity is high.

You and your friends want to start a new business. The people of Charleston love ice cream; so you will open a new ice cream store. The name of your store is The Magical Marvelous Ice Cream Company.

In your ice cream store, you will have the usual flavors of ice cream. Also, you want to have some really unusual flavors. And you want to have some marvelous sundaes for people to buy!

Prediscussion

In this discussion, you will be talking about the taste of ice cream. Study the following conversation expressions. Practice them with your teacher. Then practice them with two partners. Take turns saying how ice cream would taste, agreeing, and disagreeing.

Saying How Ice Cream Would Taste	Agreeing	Disagreeing
That sounds delicious!	It sure does.	No, it doesn't.
That would taste great!	It sure would.	No, it wouldn't.
That sounds good.	It sure does.	No, it doesn't.
That would taste good.	It sure would.	No, it wouldn't.
That sounds bad.	It sure does.	No, it doesn't.
That would taste awful.	It sure would.	No, it wouldn't.
That sounds weird.	It sure does.	No, it doesn't.
That would be strange.	It sure would.	No, it wouldn't.

People in discussions often do not understand what a person says. They must ask the person to repeat. The following expressions can be used to ask a person to repeat. Discuss and practice them with your teacher.

Asking for Repetition

Less Formal   I didn't get that. Can you repeat it please?
⬆   I didn't understand what you said.
│   Could you please repeat that?
│   Sorry, what was that again?
⬇   Excuse me. What did you say?
More Formal   Pardon me. Would you mind repeating that?

Continue practicing the expressions with your two partners. Begin with the examples.

Example 1   A: Chocolate pie ice cream sounds delicious!
              B: It sure does.
              C: No, it doesn't.

Example 2   B: Strawberry coffee would taste awful.
              A: Sorry, what was that again?
              B: I said that strawberry coffee ice cream would taste terrible.
              C: It sure would.
              A: I'm not so sure.

Example 3   C: Fried apple would taste good.
              B: No, it wouldn't.
              A: Oh, really? Why not?

Read the conversation. See how the expressions are used. Practice the conversation with a classmate.

A: I think that Vanilla-Onion Magic would taste great!
B: You've got to be kidding. Vanilla and onion? That would taste awful.
A: No, it wouldn't.
B: Come on, give me a break. Who would buy Vanilla-Onion Magic? That sounds weird.
A: Maybe it is weird, but that's why people would buy it.
B: Maybe. But they wouldn't eat it.
A: Sure they would. Think about it. People like vanilla, and people like onions. I bet that Vanilla-Onion Magic would be a hit.
B: I still don't think it would. How about Banana Cream Puff?
A: That sounds delicious!
B: It sure does. But my favorite would be Pina Colada. That would sell well.
A: It sure would. What do you think about Butter Pecan?

Decide and Write

A. Look at the following list of flavors. Put a check (✓) beside the 20 that you want to have.

strawberry

cantaloupe

____ Banana Cream Puff	____ Chocolate Chip	____ Strawberry Coffee
____ Chocolate Pie	____ Vanilla Raisin	____ Banana Nut
____ Pineapple Peppermint	____ Rocky Road	____ Peanut Butter Fudge
____ Butter Pecan	____ Caramel Cherry	____ Apple Strudel
____ Cookies and Cream	____ Orange Sherbet	____ Toasted Almond
____ Mashed Mango	____ Mocha Almond	____ Blueberry Cheesecake
____ Lemon Chocolate	____ Pina Colada	____ Rum Raisin
____ Italian Neapolitan	____ Guava Granola	____ Salted Watermelon
____ Fried Apple	____ Vanilla-Onion Magic	____ Strawberry Daiquiri
____ Peaches & Pears	____ Pralines and Cream	____ White Macadamia Nut
____ Marble Fudge	____ Peach Candy	____ Nutty Apricot

B. Create ten marvelous new flavors using parts of the above list or other fruits, nuts, creams, candies, and other items.

blackberry

pear

Flavor 1: _____

Flavor 2: _____

Flavor 3: _____

Flavor 4: _____

Flavor 5: _____

Flavor 6: _____

Flavor 7: _____

Flavor 8: _____

Flavor 9: _____

Flavor 10: _____

C. Create seven magic marvelous sundaes.

For syrup toppings, you can use butterscotch, pineapple, strawberry, chocolate, or chocolate fudge.

For nut toppings, you can use almonds, walnuts, pecans, and peanuts.

You can also use whipped cream.

guava

Sundae 1   Name: _____

Number of scoops/kinds of ice cream: _____

_____

Toppings: _____

grapes

Sundae 2   Name: _____

Number of scoops/kinds of ice cream: _____

_____

Toppings: _____

grapefruit

Sundae 3   Name: _____

Number of scoops/kinds of ice cream: _____

_____

Toppings: _____

cherry

Sundae 4   Name: _____

Number of scoops/kinds of ice cream: _____

_____

Toppings: _____

banana

apple

Sundae 5   Name: _____

Number of scoops/kinds of ice cream: _____

_____

Toppings: _____

pineapple

Sundae 6   Name: _____

Number of scoops/kinds of ice cream: _____

_____

Toppings: _____

Sundae 7   Name: _____

Number of scoops/kinds of ice cream: _____

_____

lemon

Toppings: _____

Discuss

Compare your ideas with those of other groups. Who has the best ice cream? Which sundae would you like to eat?

Extend

Written/Oral Assignment

1. Write a paragraph about desserts in your country. What are typical desserts? What kind of desserts do you like? What kind of desserts did you eat as a child?

Cultural Contact Assignment

2. If possible, visit an ice cream store or the ice cream section of a supermarket. Write down all the flavors. Discuss them with your class.

answering machine   **monitor**   **keyboard**   **disk**   **folder**

On the Job with a Green Card

Vocabulary

tuition   money for education

survive   to live

constantly   always

depressed   sad

provides   gives

permit   a special license

sexual advances   sexual talking or touching

minimum wage   lowest legal salary

tutoring   teaching privately

Read and Consider

Many international students and other non-American workers want to find a job in the United States. They need money for housing, food, tuition, and other important things.

In general, people in the United States who are not Americans must have a green card to work. A green card is a permit to work in the United States.

A green card is not easy to get. Usually one must either live in the United States for two years or marry an American citizen. There are many problems because of green cards.

You are unofficial job counselors in Houston, Texas. What do you recommend that the following people do?

Decide and Write

Before you discuss these people's situations with your group, write down a two- or three-sentence recommendation for each.

Person 1:   Sung Duk Do
          28 years old
          Korean citizen
          Married with 1 son

Sung Duk has been a Ph.D. student in Houston for four years. Next month, he is going to graduate. He wants to work in the United States for two years before he returns to Korea. He doesn't have a green card, but some of his friends from other countries have bought green cards illegally from a Houston lawyer. Sung Duk does not want to break the law, but he doesn't see any other choice. What do you recommend?

Recommendation: _____

_____

_____

_____

_____

Person 2:   Harold Dupre
          19 years old
          French citizen
          Single

Harold is in the United States on a tourist visa, but he wants to stay in the country and work. He has seen some marriage advertisements in a Houston newspaper. In these classified ads, foreign citizens offer money to Americans for marriage and a green card. Harold will pay $3000 to any woman for a marriage. He doesn't really want a wife; he just wants a green card. What do you recommend?

Recommendation: _____

_____

_____

_____

_____

_____

Person 3: Petra Smirnova
29 years old
Russian citizen
Single

Petra arrived in the United States six months ago. She is studying at Houston Community College. Her major is physics, and she is very smart. The Russian government provides her with a small amount of money every month. She has enough for housing and food—but nothing else. She doesn't have a green card, but she can make money easily by tutoring American students in mathematics and physics. What do you recommend?

Recommendation: _____

_____

_____

_____

_____

_____

Person 4: Nyugen Thieu
54 years old
Vietnamese citizen
Married, 5 children

Nyugen was a medical doctor in Vietnam. He had an excellent job with high salary and much respect. He arrived in the United States three years ago as a boat person. He has studied English for two years. However, his English is not good, and he still cannot pass the Texas medical examination. He has a special green card, but he is a hamburger cook at a fast-food restaurant. His salary is the minimum wage, his co-workers are teenagers, and his 22-year-old boss gives him no respect. Nyugen is very depressed. What should he do?

Recommendation: _____

_____

_____

_____

_____

_____

Person 5: Joachim Morales
22 years old
Mexican citizen living illegally in the United States for five years
Single

Joachim works illegally as a construction worker in Houston. He lives in an apartment with other workers and sends all of his money back to Mexico to support his parents, brothers, and sisters. Without his money, his family could not survive. Every day, Joachim is afraid the Immigration authorities will catch him. He is tired of being afraid, but he must work. What should he do?

Recommendation: _____

_____

_____

_____

_____

_____

Person 6:   Thia Larssen
            24 years old
            Swedish citizen
            Married to an American, no children

Thia has a green card and works as a computer operator for an electronics company. She makes the minimum wage and is always afraid she might lose her job. Her boss constantly tells her that there are thousands of people in her situation— and that if she makes a mistake she will lose her job. Yesterday, her boss made sexual advances toward her. What should she do?

Recommendation: _____

_____

_____

_____

_____

_____

Prediscussion

In this discussion, you will be giving advice. Study the following conversation expressions. Practice them with your teacher. Then practice them with your two partners. Fill in the blanks [. . .] with your own words. Take turns making suggestions, agreeing and disagreeing.

Making Suggestions	Agreeing	Disagreeing
If I were her, I would . . .*	So would I. Me too.	I wouldn't do that.
I believe that she should . . .	I agree.	I disagree.
I think it would be a good idea if she . . .	So do I.	I don't think so.
It might be a good idea if she . . .	I think that's a good idea.	That doesn't seem like a good idea to me.
If I were her, I wouldn't . . .*	Me either.	I would.
I don't think that she should . . .	Neither do I.	I do.

Continue practicing the expressions with your two partners. Begin with the examples.

Example 1 A: If I were Petra Smirnova, I would tutor American students.
B: So would I.
C: I wouldn't do that.
A: Why not?

Example 2 C: I don't think that Harold Dupre should get married for a green card.
B: Neither do I.
A: I do.
C: Why?

* Note that "If I were her" is used in conversation, but is not grammatical. "If I were she" is used in formal English.

Read the following discussion. See how the expressions are used. Practice the conversation with your two fellow counselors.

A: What do you think Sung Duk should do?
B: I don't think that he should buy a green card.
C: Neither do I.
A: I do.
B: Why?
A: So he can work.
C: But he might get arrested.
A: That's true, but he needs money.
B: But he can't make money in prison.
C: You're right about that.
A: Look. Everybody does it. He won't get arrested. If I were Sung Duk, I would buy the card.
B: I really disagree with you. It's too dangerous.
C: And I just don't think he should do something illegal.
B: Me either.
A: So what do you think he should do?

Discuss

Talk this over carefully in your small group. Reach agreement on what each person should do. Afterwards, compare your ideas with those of other groups.

Extend

Written/Oral Assignment

1. Look again at the problems of Nyugen Thieu and Thia Larssen (4 and 6). Choose one of them and write a conversation—either between Nyugen and his boss or between Thia and her boss. The conversation should have at least 10 to 15 sentences. Afterwards role-play the conversation in your class.

Cultural Contact Assignment

2. Go to a local McDonald's or other fast-food restaurant. Find out what is necessary to get a job, what kind of job beginners get, and how much it pays. Report on your findings to the class.

Which University Do You Want to Attend?

Vocabulary

climate   weather
humid   wet
tuition   money paid to a school for study

Read and Consider

You are an international student in the United States. For nine months, you have studied English in an excellent English program in Boston, Massachusetts. Now you speak English well enough to go to a university and study engineering—your favorite subject.

You plan to study four years and receive a B.S. in Electrical Engineering. After that, you may continue your studies or return to your country.

You are 20 years old, single, and extremely intelligent. In your country, you always made the highest grades, and, in the English program, you were the top student. You have a moderate amount of money, but you may be able to get some more. You have been accepted to seven universities. Which one will you choose?

Decide and Write

Before you discuss your ideas with your group, read the choices carefully. Put the choices in the order of your preference. Give a reason for each choice.

1. **University of Alabama:** Tuscaloosa, Alabama
   19,900 students; 1,050 teachers
   Electrical Engineering Department rated #76 in the United States
   Climate: Hot and humid in summer, cool in winter
   Cost of living: Inexpensive
   Cost of tuition: Inexpensive
   Advantage: Cousin also attends

   Order: _____

   Reason: _____

   _____

   _____

2. **Boston University:** Boston, Massachusetts
   25,000 students; 1,800 teachers
   Electrical Engineering Department rated #27 in the United States
   Climate: Cool (snows in winter)
   Cost of living: Expensive
   Cost of tuition: Expensive
   Advantage: Close to English program, not necessary to change housing and
       friends

   Order: _____

   Reason: _____

   _____

   _____

3. **University of California-Davis:** Davis, California
   24,000 students; 1,600 teachers
   Electrical Engineering Department rated #19 in the United States
   Climate: Hot in summer, moderate in winter
   Cost of living: Moderately expensive
   Cost of tuition: Moderately expensive
   Advantage: Extremely safe town

Order: _____

Reason: _____

_____

_____

4. **Drake University:** Des Moines, Iowa
   8,000 students; 270 teachers
   Electrical Engineering Department rated #92 in the United States
   Climate: Moderate (snows in winter)
   Cost of living: Very inexpensive
   Cost of tuition: Inexpensive
   Advantage: Teacher from my country teaches in Mathematics
   Department

Order: _____

Reason: _____

_____

_____

5. **University of North Carolina:** Chapel Hill, North Carolina
24,000 students; 2,000 teachers
Electrical Engineering Department rated #13 in the United States
Climate: Moderate (sometimes snows in winter)
Cost of living: Inexpensive
Cost of tuition: Moderately expensive
Advantage: Close to electrical engineering research companies

Order: _____

Reason: _____

_____

_____

6. **New Mexico State University:** Las Cruces, New Mexico
15,000 students; 800 teachers
Electrical Engineering Department rated #42 in the United States
Climate: Moderate (snows in winter)
Cost of living: Inexpensive
Cost of tuition: Inexpensive
Advantage: Electrical Engineering Department works with United States re-
    search laboratory in Los Alamos, New Mexico (one of the best in the
    United States)

Order: _____

Reason: _____

_____

_____

7. **University of Washington:** Seattle, Washington
   34,000 students; 2,900 teachers
   Electrical Engineering Department rated #39 in the United States
   Climate: Cool and wet
   Cost of living: Moderately expensive
   Cost of tuition: Moderately expensive
   Advantage: Beautiful geographic location

Order: _____

Reason: _____

_____

_____

Prediscussion

In this discussion, you will be talking to your classmates about universities. You will be giving reasons to support your opinions. Study the following conversation expressions. Practice using them with your teacher. Then practice them with a partner. Fill in the blanks [. . .] with your own words. Take turns being the person giving reasons and the person partially agreeing or disagreeing.

Giving Reasons	*Ways to Partially Agree and Disagree*
I think you should go to . . . because . . .	That's true, but . . .
One reason you should go to . . . is that . . .	That may be true, but . . .
It might be better for you to go to . . . so that . . .	I guess you're right, but . . .
I don't think you should go to . . . because . . .	That's true, but . . .
One reason you should not go to . . . is that . . .	That may be true, but . . .
It might be better for you not to go to . . . so that . . .	I guess you're right, but . . .

Continue practicing the expressions with your partner. Begin with the examples.

Example 1   A: I think you should go to Washington because it's beautiful.
              B: That's true, but the weather is rainy.

Example 2   A: One reason you should not go to the University of Alabama
                 is the weather.
              B: That may be true, but the cost of living is cheap.

Example 3   A: It might be better or you to go to the University of North
                 Carolina so that you can get a job afterwards.
              B: I guess you're right, but it's pretty expensive.

Study the following discussion. See how the expressions are used. Practice the discussion with three of your classmates. In this discussion, Person B is choosing. Persons A, C, and D are giving advice.

A: One reason you should not go to the University of Washington is that the climate is cool and wet.
B: That may be true, but the weather is bad everywhere.
C: I don't think so. The climate is moderate in Iowa, North Carolina, and New Mexico.
D: Wait a minute. Is climate the most important thing?
A: No, but it is important.
D: Well, I think a cool and wet climate is better than a hot and humid one.
C: I don't think so.
A: Me either.
B: OK. OK. Let's forget about climate.
C: That's a good idea. It might be better for you to go to the University of North Carolina so that you can get a better education.
D: I guess you're right, but why is North Carolina a better education?
A: Because its electrical engineering department is number 13 in the United States.
B: So what? I think that any department in the top 100 is good.
C: So what do you really think?
B: . . .

Discuss

For this discussion, one person is choosing the best place to go. The other people are friends. They are giving advice. Go slowly; take turns. What choice does each person make? Afterwards, share your ideas with the class.

Extend

Written/Oral Assignment

1. Write a letter to a university admissions department. Describe yourself, your educational background, your grades, and your interests. Why do you want to go to the university? Why should the university accept you?

Cultural Contact Assignment

2. If possible, go to a university admissions department in your area. Find out about admission to the university. What does a student need to do? Bring a university application form to class. How do you fill it out? Discuss these questions with your class.

tuxedo   **bowtie**   **bouquet**   **gown**   **veil**

Which Man
Should She Marry?

Vocabulary

counseling   advice
brusque   unfriendly
flirter   a person who tries to attract

Read and Consider

Approximately 2.5 million couples get married in the United States every year.
Some couples get married quickly: other couples take a long time to decide.

   You work for Rocky Mountain Marriage Counselors, Inc., located in Denver,
Colorado. Every day people come to you for marriage counseling. You try to help
them choose a husband or wife.

   Today, Susan Carson has come to you for advice. Read Susan's biography
carefully. Help her decide whom to marry.

   Susan Carson
   Age: 29 years old, Job: Policewoman ($24,000/yr.)
   Height: 5' 10", Weight: 150 lbs.
   Hobbies: Hunting, weightlifting, playing the piano
   Personality: Quiet and shy

Decide and Write

Susan believes that it is time for her to get married. She knows five men. All of the men would like to marry her. Before talking with your group, write down your individual preferences and reasons.

1. **Mike Smith**
   Age: 25, Job: Athletic Club Director ($22,000/yr.)
   Height: 6' 3", Weight: 220 lbs.
   Hobbies: Weightlifting
   Personality: Loud and social

Susan says, "I met Mike at the athletic club. We have a good time weightlifting together. He's tall and very handsome, but he's younger than me and his salary is not so great. I like his personality. I think he loves me a lot, but sometimes he still looks at other women. What do you think?"

Order: _____

Reason: _____

_____

2. **Harry Walters**
   Age: 32, Job: Bank Manager ($47,000/yr.)
   Height: 6', Weight: 170 lbs.
   Hobbies: Opera, Coin collecting
   Personality: Kind and gentle

Susan says, "I have known Harry since we were children. We grew up next door to each other. Harry is not very good-looking, but he would do anything for me. He's been asking me to marry him for ten years. He has a good job, but he wants me to quit my job because he thinks it is too dangerous. I like my job and want to keep working. What do you think?"

Order: _____

Reason: _____

_____

3. **Parviz Ghorbani**
   Age: 29, Graduate Student ($?/yr.)
   Height: 5' 11", Weight: 165 lbs.
   Hobbies: Chess, cars
   Personality: Romantic and talkative

Susan says, "I met Parviz when I gave him a speeding ticket three months ago. It was love at first sight—his eyes are so beautiful—and when I asked him why he was driving so fast, he began speaking Persian poetry. I really don't know much about him. He says he is going to be a doctor in his country after he finishes studying here. He says his family is rich. What do you think?"

Order: _____

Reason: _____

_____

4. **Paul Nelson**
   Age: 47, Job: Policeman ($42,000/yr.)
   Height: 6' 4", Weight: 195 lbs.
   Hobbies: Mountain climbing, boating
   Personality: Strong and quiet

Susan says, "Paul is my boss in the police department. I know he's a lot older than me, but he's so exciting to be with. He was married before and divorced. I like him a lot; married life with him would never be boring! He also has a very nice family, and we have a lot of the same friends. What do you think?"

Order: _____

Reason: _____

_____

5. **Adrian Tinsley**
   Age: 34, Job: Professor ($52,000/yr.)
   Height: 5' 7", Weight: 145 lbs.
   Hobbies: Reading and writing
   Personality: Quiet and brusque

Susan says, "Of all the men I know, Adrian is the smartest. I met him when I took a criminology class at the University of Colorado. He's very difficult to get to know so he doesn't have any friends. I think he likes me because I understand him. He's handsome and dresses very well. What do you think?"

Order: _____

Reason: _____

_____

Prediscussion

In this discussion, you will be talking about the best man for Susan to marry. Study the following conversation expressions. Practice using them with your teacher. Then practice them with a partner. Fill in the blanks [. . .] with your own words. Take turns giving an opinion and asking a response question.

Giving an Opinion

I think that . . . would be a good choice.
In my opinion, . . . would make a good husband.
I believe that Susan and . . . would be a good match.

I don't think that . . . would be a good choice.
In my opinion, . . . would not make a good husband.
I don't believe that Susan and . . . would be a good match.

Response Questions

Why?
Why do you think that?
Why do you say that?

Why not?
Why do you think that?
Why do you say that?

Continue practicing the expressions with your partner. Begin with the examples.

Example 1 A: I think that Paul Nelson would be a good choice.
B: Why do you say that?
A: Because they work together.

Example 2 A: In my opinion, Parviz Ghorbani would make a good husband.
B: Why do you think that?
A: Because he's rich.

Example 3 A: I don't believe that Susan and Harry would be a good match.
B: Why not?
A: Because they would have job problems.

Study the following discussion. See how the expressions are used. Practice the discussion with two of your classmates.

A: In my opinion, none of these guys would make a good husband.
B: Why not?
A: Because none of them is exactly right.
C: Well let's take them one at a time. Who do you want to start with?
A: How about the first one, Mike Smith?
B: OK. So what's his problem?
A: For one thing, he's almost five years younger than she is.
B: So?
A: So, the age difference is too much. And the man should be older.
C: Why do you say that?
A: Because women get older faster than men.
C: No way. That's nonsense.
B: I don't think so either.
A: Well, what do **you** think about Mike Smith?
B: I believe that Susan and Mike might make a good match.
C: Why do you think that?
B: They have the same interests.
A: That's true, but he's a flirt. I don't think he really loves Susan.
C: Me either. Let's move on to the next guy.

Discuss

In a small group, choose the best husband for Susan Carson. Rank the men in the order of your preference. All of the group members must agree on the order.

Compare your ideas with those of your classmates. Listen carefully to the differences between men and women. Do you agree or disagree with your classmates?

Extend

Written/Oral Assignment

1. With a partner, write a conversation between a man and a woman. In the conversation, one of the people will propose marriage. The people will talk about personality, job, physical appearance, and other important factors. Role-play the conversation for the class.

Cultural Contact Assignment

2. Talk to at least three Americans. Ask them to rank the following factors in importance when finding a marriage partner. When you have the results, report them to the class.

(1 = most important, 8 = least important; if the person mentions something not on the list, use the "other" blank.)

	American 1	American 2	American 3
Family	_____	_____	_____
Religion	_____	_____	_____
Intelligence	_____	_____	_____
Job (Salary)	_____	_____	_____
Physical Appearance	_____	_____	_____
Personality	_____	_____	_____
Race/Native Country	_____	_____	_____
Interest/Hobbies	_____	_____	_____
(Other)	_____	_____	_____

| placemat | salad plate | plate | knife | spoon | cup | saucer | serving dish | salad fork | fork | napkin | candlestick | water glass | wine glass |

Plan the Perfect Dinners

Vocabulary

catering   giving food to
promotion   a better job
mood   feeling
unsuitable   not good for
impress   to give a high opinion

Read and Consider

Many times people discuss important subjects as they eat dinner. Sometimes they talk about business; sometimes they talk about love; sometimes they talk about family matters.

Your group works for the Happy Catering Company of Ann Arbor, Michigan. Your job is to provide "perfect" dinners for customers.

Tonight Happy Catering is catering two dinners. To the first dinner, a woman has invited her boss and her boss's wife. At the dinner, she wants to ask for a promotion. To the second dinner, a man has invited his girlfriend. At the dinner, he will propose marriage to her.

Prediscussion

In this discussion, you will be talking about the eating situation and the food. Study the following conversation expressions. Practice using them with your teacher. Then practice using them with a partner. Take turns being the person talking about appropriateness and the person positively or negatively agreeing.

Talking About Appropriateness

I think that the lighting matches the mood.
I believe that the lighting is appropriate
    for the occasion.
I think the seating arrangement goes
    with the situation.

Positive Agreeing

You're absolutely right!
I couldn't agree more!
Great idea.
Definitely.
You can say that again.

You're right about that.
You're right.
I agree.
I think so too.
You've got a good point there.
Good point.
Good idea.
That makes sense.
Me too.
So do I.
I do too.
I see what you mean.
That's true.

That seems like a good idea.
I guess that's a good idea.
I guess so.
Maybe so.
Maybe.

Talking About Inappropriateness

I don't think that bright light matches
    the romantic mood.
I don't believe that rock music is
    appropriate for a business dinner.
I don't think that wonton soup goes
    with macaroni and cheese.

Negative Agreeing

No, it doesn't (isn't).
I don't think so either.
Neither do I.
Me either.
You can say that again.
You're right about that.
You're right.
I agree.
You've got a good point there.
Good point.
I see what you mean.
That's true.
I guess not.
Maybe not.

Continue practicing the expressions with your partner. Begin with the examples.

Example 1   A: What kind of salad goes with the shrimp dip?
              B: I think that Caesar salad goes with shrimp dip.
              A: Why?

Example 2   B: What kind of lighting is the most romantic?
              A: I think that soft lighting matches the mood.
              B: Why not candles?

Study the following discussion. See how the expressions are used. Practice the discussion with two of your classmates.

A: What kind of lighting is the most romantic?
B: I think that soft lighting matches the mood.
C: I don't think so. Candles are more romantic.
B: Why?
C: Because candles give less light.
A: That's true, and there is something romantic about fire.
B: There is something romantic about fire?
A: Yes.
B: What?
C: Well, for one thing, fire is warm.
B: And dangerous. What would happen if the candle turned over?
A: Come on. Give me a break. You just don't like candles. Anyway it's two
    against one. I guess the candles win.
B: All right, but I still like soft lighting better.

Decide and Write

Talk over each dinner situation carefully with your group, and decide on the details.

Dinner 1
Situation: A woman asking her boss for a promotion
Number of diners: 4 (the woman, her husband, the boss, the boss's wife)

Circle the best choice for each of the following considerations.

I. Nonfood considerations

    A. Mood
        1. Romantic
        2. Professional
        3. Funny
        4. Very serious

    B. Eating place
        1. Kitchen
        2. Living room
        3. Dining room
        4. Den in front of fireplace
        5. Outside balcony

    C. Table shape
        1. No table (eat on floor on pillows)
        2. Round
        3. Square

    D. Seating arrangement
        1. Woman sits beside boss on left side
        2. Woman sits beside boss on right side
        3. Woman sits beside boss's wife
        4. Woman sits across from boss

    E. Lighting
        1. Bright
        2. Soft
        3. Candles

F. Music
  1. Rock
  2. No music
  3. Classical
  4. Romantic

II. Food

A. Hors d'oeuvre
  1. Nut cheese balls
  2. Stuffed cucumbers
  3. Chopped goose liver
  4. Caviar
  5. Shrimp dip

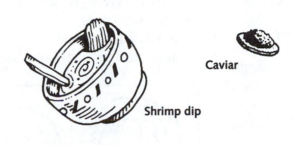

Caviar

Shrimp dip

B. Salad
  1. Caesar salad
  2. Bean salad
  3. Potato salad
  4. Regular tossed salad
  5. Chicken salad

Tossed salad

Caesar salad

C. Fruit
  1. Cinnamon apples
  2. Baked bananas
  3. Strawberries and cream
  4. Grapefruit cups
  5. Cantaloupe

Cantaloupe

Strawberries and cream

D. Soup
  1. Wonton
  2. French onion
  3. Fish chowder
  4. Creamy mushroom
  5. Lentil

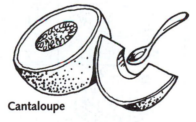

Wonton soup

Mushroom soup

E. Rice and pasta
  1. Wild rice
  2. Chinese fried rice
  3. Spanish rice
  4. Macaroni and cheese
  5. Spaghetti

Wild rice

Spanish rice

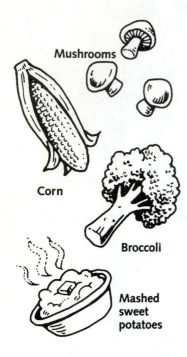

Mushrooms

Corn

Broccoli

Mashed
sweet
potatoes

F. Vegetables (choose 3)
1. Baked cabbage
2. Creamed broccoli
3. Sauteed cauliflower
4. Corn on the cob
5. Steamed mushrooms
6. Boiled green peas
7. Onions and green peppers
8. Scalloped potatoes
9. Mashed sweet potatoes
10. Spinach, tomato, and cheese loaf

Cabbage	Cauliflower	Potatoes
Sweet Potatoes	Green beans	Onions
Spinach	Bell peppers	Tomatoes

G. Main course (Choose 2)
    1. Baked stuffed lobster
    2. Shrimp teriyaki
    3. T-bone steak
    4. Beef stroganoff
    5. Curried lamb
    6. Barbecued pork ribs
    7. Fried chicken
    8. Sweet and sour pork
    9. Broiled turkey
    10. Duck with oranges

Turkey   Lobster   T-bone steak

H. Dessert
    1. Chocolate cake
    2. Strawberry ice cream
    3. Apple pie
    4. Lemon meringue pie
    5. Blueberry cheesecake
    6. Fruit salad
    7. Chocolate chip cookies

Cake   Apple pie

Cookie   Fruit salad

I. Drinks during meal (Choose 2)
    1. Mineral water
    2. Soft drink
    3. Iced tea
    4. White wine
    5. Red wine
    6. Beer
    7. Apple juice
    8. Orange juice

Red wine   Coffee

Soft drink

J. Drinks after meal (Choose 2)
    1. Coffee
    2. Tea
    3. Hot apple juice
    4. Sherry
    5. Brandy

Tea

Hot apple juice

Dinner 2
Situation: A man proposing marriage to his girlfriend
Number of diners: 2

Fill in the blanks with your ideas. You can use items from the list for Dinner 1, or you can use your own ideas (and foods).

I. Nonfood considerations

  A. Mood: _____

  B. Eating place: _____

  C. Table shape: _____

  D. Seating arrangement: _____

  E. Lighting: _____

  F. Music: _____

II. Food

  A. Hors d'oeuvre: _____

  B. Salad: _____

  C. Fruit: _____

  D. Soup: _____

  E. Rice and/or pasta: _____

  F. Vegetables: _____

  G. Main course: _____

  H. Dessert: _____

  I. Drinks during dinner: _____

  J. Drinks after dinner: _____

Discuss

After you finish discussing these situations with your group, discuss them with your entire class. What ideas did your classmates come up with? Whom do you think made the most "perfect" meal?

Extend

Written/Oral Assignment

1. Make a list of every item of food and drink you consume during the next two days. Use the following chart. Afterwards, compare your chart with those of three of your classmates. What similarities and differences do you see? Discuss your findings with your class.

	Food	Drink
Day 1		
Day 2		

Cultural Contact Assignment

2. Go to a local restaurant. If possible, get a take-out menu from the restaurant and bring it to class. If this is not possible, look at the menu on the outside of the restaurant. Write down ten different items on the menu—with their prices. Discuss the restaurant with your class. What kind of food does it have? Is it cheap or expensive? Would you like to eat there?

Doctor's Orders

Read and Consider

When a person is very sick, he or she must go to a doctor for treatment and medicine. For example, a person needs medicine for a high fever or a painful ear infection. On the other hand, doctors are not needed for minor aches and sicknesses.

You are a group of doctors at Milwaukee Memorial Hospital in Milwaukee, Wisconsin. Every day many people come to the emergency room of the hospital who do not really need to come. You have decided to write a small pamphlet about how to treat minor aches, pains, and other medical problems.

Decide and Write

Before discussing these problems with your fellow doctors, write down an appropriate treatment for each one.

Problem 1: **Headache**

Treatment: _____

_____

Problem 2: **Eye pain** (either "tired" eyes or "red" eyes)

Treatment: _____

_____

Problem 3: **Earache**

Treatment: _____

_____

Problem 4: **Toothache**

Treatment: _____

_____

Problem 5: **Sore throat**

Treatment: _____

_____

Problem 6: **A cold**

Treatment: _____

_____

Problem 7: **A low fever**

Treatment: _____

_____

Problem 8: **Cold sores in or around the mouth**

Treatment: _____

_____

Problem 9: **Minor coughing**

Treatment: _____

_____

Problem 10: **General muscle pains (back, shoulders, arms, legs)**

Treatment: _____

_____

Problem 11: **Stomachache (upset stomach)**

Treatment: _____

_____

Problem 12: **Constipation**

Treatment: _____

_____

Problem 13: **Diarrhea**

Treatment: _____

_____

Problem 14: **Sprained knee, ankle, or wrist**

Treatment: _____

_____

Problem 15: **Simple cut or scratch**

Treatment: _____

_____

Problem 16: **Nosebleed**

Treatment: _____

_____

Problem 17: **Minor burn**

Treatment: _____

_____

Problem 18: **Insomnia (can't sleep)**

Treatment: _____

_____

Problem 19: **Overweight**

Treatment: _____

_____

Prediscussion

In this discussion, your group will be talking about making people feel better. Study the following expressions. Practice using them with your teacher. Fill in the blanks [. . .] with your own words.

Talking About Feeling Better

The best thing to do is . . .
The person would feel better if she . . .
The person may feel better if she . . .
The person might feel better if she . . .

. . . would not help the person at all.
. . . would not be the best thing to do.
. . . would/may/might not make the person feel better.

Continue practicing the expressions with a partner. Begin with the examples.

Example 1   A: The best thing to do for a headache is to take a hot shower.
B: Taking a shower would not be the best thing to do.
A: Why not?

Example 2   B: The person who can't sleep might feel better if she drank some warm milk before going to bed.
A: Drinking some warm milk would not help the person at all.
B: Why not?

Example 3   A: A person who has a low fever would feel better if she slept a lot and drank a lot of orange juice.
B: That seems like a good idea.
A: How much should she sleep and drink?

Study the following discussion. See how the expressions are used. Practice the discussion with two of your classmates.

A: What do you think that a person who has a low fever should do?

B: A person who has a low fever would feel better if she rested a lot and drank a lot of orange juice.

A: That seems like a good idea, but how much should she sleep and how much should she drink?

B: A lot.

C: Please be more specific.

A: Well, I think the person might feel better if she slept ten hours a day and drank two liters of orange juice a day.

B: That's a lot of orange juice.

A: Not really. The person needs a lot of fluid.

B: And what happens if she doesn't feel better?

C: Then she should go to the doctor.

B: For a low fever?

A: It might be serious. After a week of low fever, she definitely should go to the doctor.

Discuss

After you discuss the treatment of these problems in your small group of "doctors," compare your answers with the other "doctors" in the classroom. Which "medical" group would you go to?

Extend

Written/Oral Assignment

1. With a partner, write a conversation between a patient and a doctor. The patient has a sore throat, a stopped-up nose, and a fever. The doctor must examine the patient, find out the problem, and prescribe some medicine. The patient is not very nice, and the doctor isn't either.

   When you finish, exchange conversations with another pair. Make corrections if necessary. Role-play the other group's conversation for the class.

Cultural Contact Assignment

2. Go to a campus clinic, hospital, or doctor's office.
   Find out what a person must do before seeing a doctor.

Redesigning the Wheel?

Vocabulary

redesign remake
inventors people who make new things

Read and Consider

New inventions are made all the time. Also, many "old" items such as tennis shoes, light bulbs, radios, toothbrushes, and sunglasses are changed to make them better.

Some items, however, have never changed very much. You are a group of inventors in Rutgers, New Jersey. You have decided that it is time to redesign some of these basic items to make them easier to use. Because these are designs, you must draw sketches of the new objects.

Prediscussion

In this discussion, you will be talking about how things look and how they work. Study the following expressions. Practice using them with your teacher.

Saying How Something Will Look or Work

Strong Yes   It looks good.
              It will work well.

              I think that it looks good.
              I think that it will work well.

              I believe that it looks OK.
              I believe that it will work OK.

              I don't think that it looks good.
              I don't think that it will work well.

              It doesn't look good.
Strong No   It won't work well.

Continue practicing the expressions with a partner. Begin with the examples.

Example 1   A: What do you think about my new pencil?
              B: I think that it looks good, but I don't think it will work well.
              A: Why not?

Example 2   B: What do you think about my new tennis racket?
              A: It doesn't look good, and I don't think it will work very well either.
              B: Why not?

Study the following discussion. See how the expressions are used. Practice the conversation with two of your fellow inventors.

A: What do you think about my new tennis racket?

B: It doesn't look good, and it won't work.

C: I believe that it looks OK, but I don't think it will work either.

A: Why not?

B: How can you hit the ball? The strings are on the handle.

A: You don't understand.

C: I guess I don't understand either.

A: The strings are not on the handle. There is no handle.

B: So how do you hit the ball?

A: With the strings. The whole racket is just two sets of strings.

C: It looks more like a butterfly than a tennis racket.

B: Well, let me repeat myself. It doesn't look good, and it won't work.

C: I still think it looks OK, but I don't think it will work.

A: OK, OK. Let's see your tennis rackets!

Decide and Draw

Item 1: **Wooden pencil**

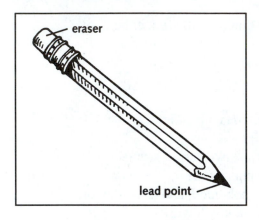

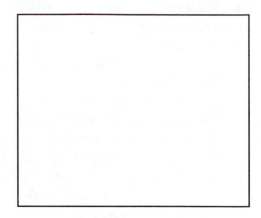

Item 2: **Clothes hanger**

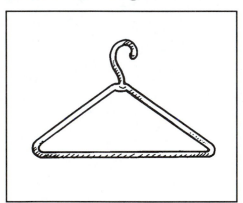

Item 3: **Soft drink can**

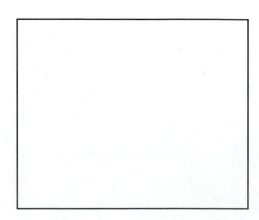

Item 4: **Fork**

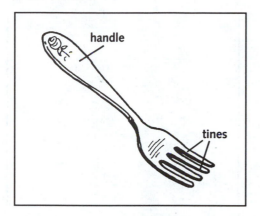

Item 5: **Pair of glasses**

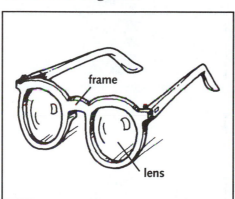

Item 6: **Pair of scissors**

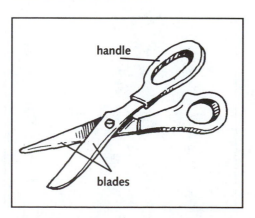

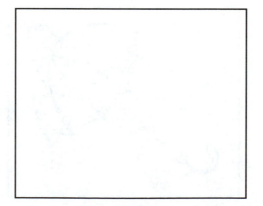

Item 7: **Hammer**

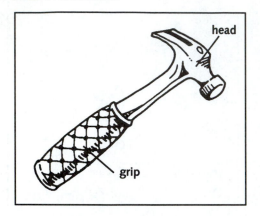

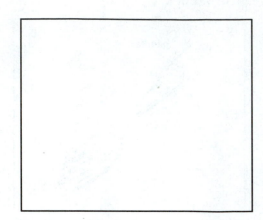

Item 8: **Tennis racket**

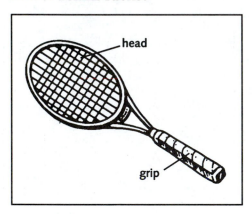

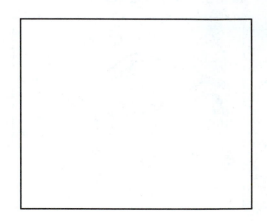

Item 9: **Umbrella**

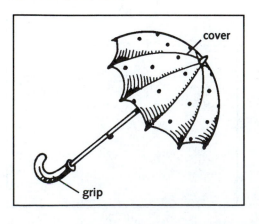

Item 10: **Match**

Discuss

When your group has finished its drawings, mix them with the drawings from other groups and pin them on a board or wall. Let everyone vote on the best design of each item.

Extend

Written/Oral Assignment

1. Choose one other item to redesign. Make a drawing of it, and bring it to class. Show the picture to the class, and explain how it works.

Cultural Contact Assignment

2. Take a short walk with your class. What interestingly designed items do you see (buildings, cars, bikes, and other items)? Discuss with your class.

What Would You Do If?

Vocabulary

unexpected   surprising

speeding   driving too fast

officer   police person

bill   amount of money owed

check on   to find out about

suspicious   possibly dangerous

screaming   crying loudly

grabs   holds strongly

Read and Consider

You are members of the tourist department of the New Zealand embassy in Washington, D.C. Over fifty thousand New Zealanders visited the United States last year. This year the number will probably be sixty thousand.

Unexpected situations often happen to visitors from other countries. Your department has decided to write a book to give to New Zealand tourists. In this book, you are going to tell the tourists what to do when unexpected situations happen.

Decide and Write

Before you discuss your ideas with the rest of your department, write them in the blanks. For each situation, write down three different actions a tourist should take.

Situation A: A tourist is driving a rental car down a Virginia freeway. Her speed is 80 miles per hour, but the speed limit is 65 miles per hour. She is stopped by the Virginia State Police for speeding. The officer starts to give her a ticket. What should the tourist do?

1. _____

2. _____

3. _____

Situation B: A tourist has been staying in a New Orleans hotel for one week. When he checks out, he receives a telephone bill for $550. The tourist did not make any of the phone calls, but the hotel says he did. What should the tourist do?

1. _____

2. _____

3. _____

Situation C: A tourist is walking down a street in San Francisco. A man walks up to her, says he is homeless, grabs her arm, and asks her for money. What should the tourist do?

1. _____

2. _____

3. _____

Situation D: A tourist is riding on a train between Fargo, North Dakota, and St. Louis, Missouri. On the train, he meets an interesting woman. She is very nice to him and invites him to stay in her apartment in St. Louis. What should the tourist do?

1. _____

2. _____

3. _____

Situation E: A tourist couple is eating in a restaurant in Portland, Oregon. They order dinner. After 35 minutes, their food has not arrived. Other people who sat down after them receive their food. They ask the waiter about their food. They wait another 30 minutes. What should the tourists do?

1. _____

2. _____

3. _____

Situation F: It is late at night in Orlando, Florida. A tourist takes a taxi from the Disneyworld disco to her hotel. After she gets out of the taxi and the taxi leaves, she sees a suspicious man between her and the hotel. There is no one else on the street. What should the tourist do?

1. _____

2. _____

3. _____

Situation G: A tourist is walking down the boardwalk in Atlantic City, New Jersey. He finds twenty $1,000 bills on the street. What should the tourist do?

1. _____

2. _____

3. _____

Situation H: A tourist couple is driving alone in a car in Providence, Rhode Island. In front of them there is a terrible accident between two cars. Inside one of the cars a woman is screaming for help. She is bleeding very badly. It is late at night, and no one else is around. What should the tourists do?

1. _____

2. _____

3. _____

Situation I: A tourist is shopping in a Boise, Idaho, bookstore. When she walked in, she left her backpack with all of her money, credit cards, and identification (including a passport) on a shelf near the door. When she finishes shopping, she finds out that her backpack is gone. She asks a store clerk to help her, but the clerk says it is not the bookstore's responsibility. What should the tourist do?

1. _____

2. _____

3. _____

Prediscussion

In this discussion, you will be talking about tourists. What should they do? What shouldn't they do? Study the following conversation expressions. Practice using the expressions with your teacher. Then practice using them with two of your classmates. Fill in the blanks [. . .] with your own words. Take turns saying what tourists should or should not do, agreeing, and disagreeing.

Saying What Tourists *Should or Should Not Do*	*Agreeing*	*Disagreeing*
I think the tourist should . . .	So do I.	I don't.
I think the tourist ought to . . .	Me too.	I don't think so.
I think it would be a good idea if the tourist . . .	I think so too.	I don't think so.
I don't think the tourist should . . .	Neither do I.	I do.
I don't think the tourist ought to . . .	Me either.	I do.

I don't think it would be a
    good idea for the tourist to . . .
	I don't think
	    so either.
		I think it would be.

Continue practicing the expressions with your two partners. Begin with the examples.

Example 1   A: I think the tourist should pretend to speak no English.
              B: So do I.
              C: I don't think so.

Example 2 B: I don't think it would be a good idea for the tourist to pretend to speak no English.

A: I don't think so either.

C: I think it would be.

Study the following discussion. See how the expressions are used. Practice the discussion with your two classmates.

A: I think the tourist should pretend to speak no English.

B: So do I. Maybe the officer won't give her a ticket.

C: I don't think so. I tried it one time, and it didn't work. I think it would be a good idea if the tourist was very nice and told the officer that the United States is a great country.

A: You've got to be kidding.

C: No, I'm serious. It might work.

B: I don't think so. I think the officer would give her a bigger ticket.

C: So what do you suggest?

B: I think the tourist ought to say nothing and take the ticket.

A: Me too.

C: That's a good idea.

Discuss

Share your ideas with the rest of your "department." Try to agree on the best ideas to tell the tourists. Afterwards, compare your ideas with those of other groups. Listen carefully for ideas that are different from yours.

Extend

Written/Oral Assignment

1. Choose two of the above situations and write a conversation based on each of them. For example, you might write a conversation between a tourist and a policeman, and between a tourist and a homeless person. Practice the conversations with a partner and perform them for the class.

Cultural Contact Assignment

2. If possible, go on a field trip to a campus police station, or go individually to a police station or court. Write down your observations and share them with the class.

What Will We Do with the Park?

Vocabulary

types   kinds

resources   valuable things

timber   wood

employ   to hire

commission   a group of people who perform a duty

pump out   to take

mine   to dig out

export   to send out of the country

Read and Consider

Alaska is the largest state in the United States. It also has the largest state parks. Notaki State Park is a large Alaskan park. It has about 7,000 square miles.

Eskimos have lived in Notaki for thousands of years. It is also the home of hundreds of types of animals, including bears, moose, wolves, caribou, and salmon. Notaki also has many natural resources. The park is covered with forests. Oil and gold have been found there.

Many groups want to use Notaki. You are members of the Alaska Park Commission in Juneau, Alaska. You must decide how to use the park.

Decide and Write

Study the following map. Read what each group wants to do. Decide what is best for Alaska and for Notaki. Before discussing this with your group, write down your decisions and reasons.

NOTAKI

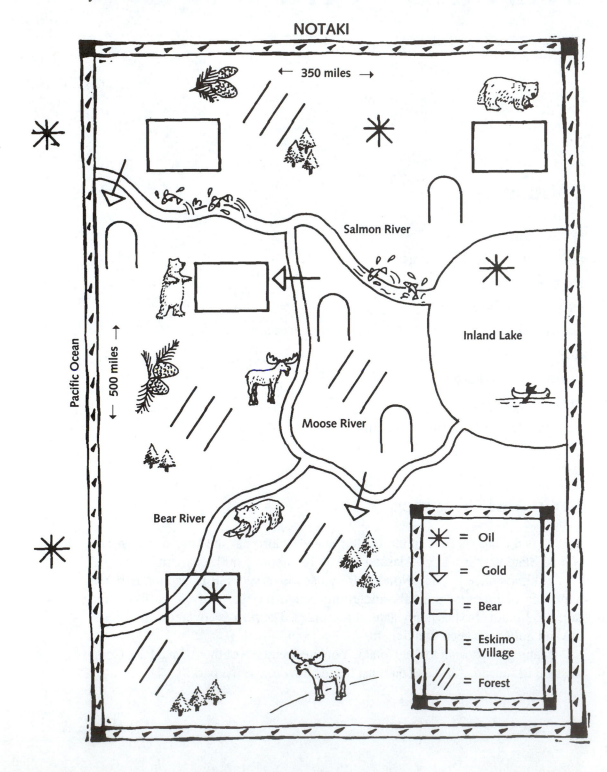

Group 1: **Shell Oil Co.**

Shell has already spent $987 million dollars finding oil in Notaki. The company wants permission to find more oil and to pump out all of the oil it has found.

Your decision and reasons: _____

_____

_____

_____

Group 2: **The Alaska Game and Fish Department**

This department helps Alaskan hunters and fishermen. It wants permission for hunters to kill bears and moose in Notaki, and it wants for non-Eskimos to be able to fish for salmon. The department does not want oil, gold, or timber taken out of the park.

Your decision and reasons: _____

_____

_____

_____

Group 3: **The Klondike Gold Co.**

This company wants permission to mine the gold in Notaki. It will pay the state 25 percent of its profits and employ about four hundred workers.

Your decision and reasons: _____

_____

_____

_____

Group 4: **The Sierra Club**

This environmental group tries to protect animals and land throughout the United States. It does not want any changes in Notaki. It does not want any oil, gold, or timber taken from the park, and it does not want any more hunting and fishing (except for Eskimos).

Your decision and reasons: _____

_____

_____

_____

Group 5: **Northwest Pacific Lumber Co. and Habashi Lumber Co.**

These two companies want permission to cut down the trees in Notaki. They will pay the state of Alaska $1 per tree (a total of about $100 million) and $50 million more for permission to export the timber to Japan.

Your decision and reasons: _____

_____

_____

_____

Group 6: **The Eskimos**

The Eskimos do not want any trees or gold taken from Notaki. They do not want oil taken from the land or the lake in the park. They do support taking oil from off the coast—if they receive 50 percent of all profits. They don't want any hunting or fishing by non-Eskimos.

Your decision and reasons: _____

_____

_____

_____

Prediscussion

In this discussion, you will be talking about giving permission. Your language will be formal. Study the following conversation expressions. Practice using them with your teacher. Fill in the blanks [. . .] with your own words.

To Favor Complete Permission

I agree completely with their position. We should give them permission to . . .
I think they're right. We should give them permission to . . .
I believe they're correct. We should allow them to . . .

To Favor Partial Permission

I somewhat agree with their position. We should give them partial permission to . . .
I think they're partly right. We should give them partial permission to . . .
I believe they're partly correct. We should give them partial permission to . . .

To Favor No Permission

I disagree completely with their position. We should not give them permission to . . .
I think they're completely wrong. We should not allow them to . . .
I believe they're absolutely incorrect. We should not permit them to . . .

People in small discussion groups often interrupt each other. The following expressions can be used to interrupt. Discuss these expressions with your teacher.

Interrupting

Casual	Wait a minute, I think that . . .
↑	Un-hunh, that reminds me . . .
	Yeah, I'd just like to say that . . .
	Sorry to interrupt you, but . . .
↓	Excuse me, may I interrupt you for a minute?
Polite	Ummm, excuse me, may I say something?

After a speaker has been interrupted, she or he will often return to her or his idea. The following expressions can be used to return to an idea. Discuss how these expressions are used with your teacher.

Returning to an Idea

Well, anyway . . .
Well, as I started to say . . .
As I was saying . . .
Now where was I? . . .
Well, moving back to the subject . . .

Continue practicing the expressions with a partner. Begin with the examples.

> *Example 1* A: What do you think about the Klondike Gold Company's idea?
> B: I agree completely with their position. We should give them permission to mine the gold. In fact, I think Klondike is one of the best companies in Alaska. Last year . . .
> A: Sorry to interrupt you, but Klondike is not such a great company. They have destroyed many places in our state. Don't you agree?
> B: Well, as I started to say, last year they changed the company.

> *Example 2* B: What do you think about the Klondike Gold Company's idea?
> A: I think they're partly right. We should give them partial permission to mine the gold.

Study the following discussion. See how the expressions are used. Practice the discussion with three of your classmates.

A: What do you think about Shell's idea?
B: I somewhat agree with their position. We should give them partial permission to look for oil.
C: Have you forgotten about the oil pollution in Alaska?
D: I haven't. The oil in the ocean killed thousands of animals.
B: Well, I haven't forgotten either, but Shell provides money and jobs to Alaska. I said that "I somewhat agree" with their position.
A: I think you're right. Shell did not cause the pollution.
C: I think both of you are completely wrong. We should not allow Shell to do anything!
D: I agree. We should not give them any permission.
A: So what are we going to do? Two of us want to give Shell partial permission and two of us don't want to give any permission.
B: Let's . . .

Discuss

All of your group must agree on each decision. Each decision must be very specific—especially if you give partial permission.

Put a map of Notaki on the board, and discuss your group's ideas with the rest of the class. What similarities and differences do you see among the ideas?

Extend

Written/Oral Assignment

1. Write a letter to the Alaska Park Commission. In the letter, explain how you feel about Notaki, and what you think the commission should do.

Cultural Contact Assignment

2. Find a map of a geographical area of the United States. (If you are in the United States, one that is close to you). What state and national parks do you see? If possible, visit a state or national park and share your experiences with the class.

What's In
and What's Not?

Vocabulary

editors   people who make books and magazines

"in"   popular

average   regular

articles   stories

"out"   not popular

Read and Consider

You are the editors of *Popularity* magazine in New York City. Your magazine tries to have articles and photographs about the most popular items in American culture.

Today, the managing editor of *Popularity* has given you a list of 40 items. You need to decide if they are "in" or "out." After you decide, your editor wants you to compare some of your opinions with those of other "average" Americans.

Prediscussion

In this discussion, you will be giving your opinions about popularity. Is the item popular or not? You will use some slang. Study the following conversation expressions. Practice using the expressions with your teacher. Then practice using them with a classmate. Take turns describing popularity, agreeing, and disagreeing.

	Describing Popularity	*Agreeing*
Very Popular	In!	You're absolutely right.
	That's definitely in.	I couldn't agree more.
	Hey, that's really popular.	Definitely.
	That's popular.	You can say that again.
	That's pretty popular.	
	That's not so popular.	You're right about that.
	Hey, that's really out.	You're right.
	That's definitely history.	I agree.
Not Popular	Out!	I think so too.

I guess so.
Maybe so.
I'm not so sure.

Disagreeing

Come on, give me a break.*
You've got to be kidding.*
No way.*

I disagree.
I don't think so.

I kind of disagree.
Really?

*Remember that these may be considered impolite.

Continue practicing the expressions with your partner. Begin with the examples.

Example 1   A: So what do you think about Madonna?
             B: She's definitely in.
             A: No way, she's definitely history.

Example 2   B: What about MTV?
             A: In!
             B: Definitely.

Study the following discussion. See how the expressions are used. Practice the discussion with two of your classmates.

A: Well, what do you think about Sylvester Stallone?
B: He's history.
C: No way.
A: I think he's really out.
C: How can you say that? What about *Rocky* and *Rambo*?
B: That's what I mean. *Rocky* and *Rambo* were years ago.
C: He's made other movies since then.
A: Like what?
C: Well, I can't remember the names of any.
B: So he's out.
C: Well, maybe.

Decide and Write

You editors must agree on each item or person. Be sure to give reasons to support your opinion. Make sure that each person in the group knows what the item is or who the person is. Put one of the following symbols beside each item or person.

* = in
? = not in and not out
- = out

1. ____ Madonna		16. ____ short skirts
2. ____ MTV		17. ____ English language
3. ____ video games		18. ____ European clothes
4. ____ men's earrings		19. ____ Levi jeans
5. ____ bikinis		20. ____ Nike shoes
6. ____ Nintendo Gameboy		21. ____ pizza
7. ____ American cars		22. ____ rap music
8. ____ Sylvester Stallone		23. ____ cigarettes
9. ____ Arnold Schwarzenegger		24. ____ tattoos
10. ____ the dollar		25. ____ CDs
11. ____ Julio Iglesias		26. ____ Michael Jackson
12. ____ tennis		27. ____ Japanese cars
13. ____ Mel Gibson		28. ____ nose rings
14. ____ rock music		29. ____ Reebok shoes
15. ____ German cars		30. ____ men's long hair

Discuss

After you have chosen what's in and what's out, discuss the preceding list with your class. Then try to come up with a class list of the 20 most "in" items and people (either from the preceding list or not).

Extend

Written/Oral Assignment and Cultural Contact Assignment

Intercultural Research Project

For this project, you will need to talk to at least five Americans. Try to choose as many different people as you can: old people, young people, women, men, African-Americans, white, Native American, Asian, Hispanic.

First, fill out the personal information form for each person. Then ask the questions. (You might want to practice this in class before actually talking to Americans.)

When you have obtained the information, write down your results in a composition.

Form

Name: _____ Male/Female: _____

Approximate Age: ____ Job: _____

Questions

1. Who is the most popular actor and actress now?
2. Who is the most popular singing group?
3. What kinds of clothes are the most "in"?
4. What do you like to eat the most: sushi, pizza, tacos, or hamburgers?
5. Which cars do you think are the best: German cars, American cars, or Japanese cars?
6. What would you rather do: play a computer game, watch TV, read a book, or play with a Nintendo Gameboy?
7. What do you like to receive the most: letters or faxes?
   What do you like to send the most: letters or faxes?
8. What's your favorite drink?
9. If you could choose one country to live in—other than the United States—what would it be?
10. Please name something that is really "in" right now.

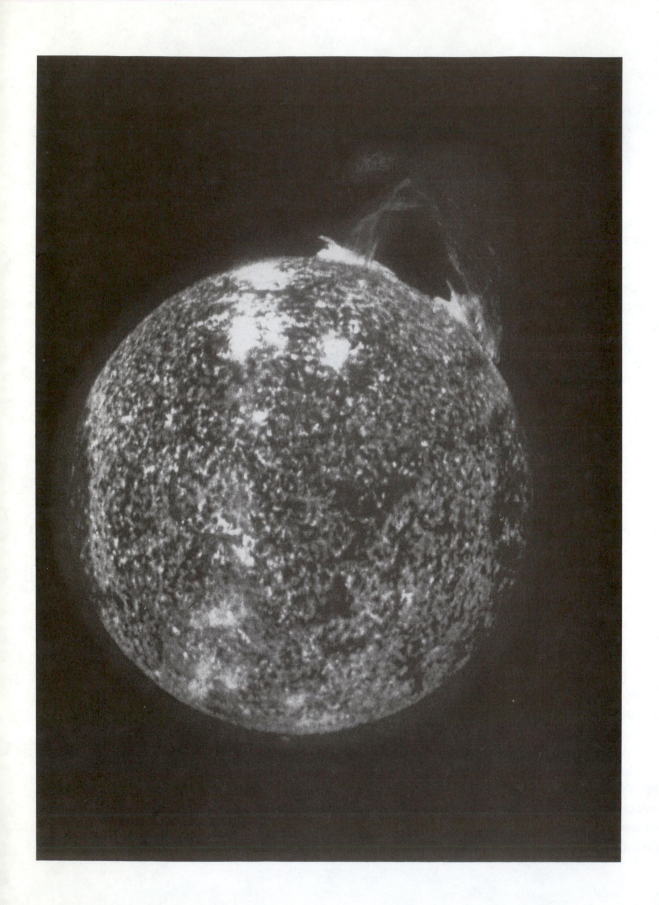

The World
is Coming to an End!

Vocabulary

run out of   to become empty

explode   to blow up

field   area

commit suicide   to kill oneself

disaster   terrible event

Read and Consider

The year is 2759. The sun is running out of fuel. It will probably explode in six months. If the sun explodes, the Earth will burn up, and everyone will die. Scientists, however, are still looking for a way to stop the coming disaster.

People all over the world are getting crazy. The police cannot control the situation. The world is becoming more dangerous every day.

Your family lives in Pittsburgh, Pennsylvania. Your family consists of a grandmother (67), a father (44), a mother (43), and two children (9,7). The grandmother is retired. The father is a computer scientist, and the mother is one of the world's top research scientists in the field of astronomy.

What do you think the family should do during the last six months?

Decide and Write

Before discussing this problem with your group, read the options carefully, order them, and write down a reason for your choice.

Choice A: Do nothing special. Continue living as now. Try not to worry about the situation because you can do nothing about it.

Order: _____

Reason: _____

_____

Choice B: Continue living as normally as possible. Take all of your family to see a family psychologist for help about the situation.

Order: _____

Reason: _____

_____

Choice C: Have the mother and father quit their jobs and take the children out of school. The family should spend all of its remaining time together.

Order: _____

Reason: _____

_____

Choice D: Continue living as normally as possible for three months. During the last three months, sell everything and take a trip around the world.

Order: _____

Reason: _____

_____

Choice E: Commit suicide. Avoid the final, crazy, dangerous last six months.

Order: _____

Reason: _____

_____

Choice F: Become more religious. Spend your time praying that the sun will not explode and that the Earth will not be destroyed.

Order: _____

Reason: _____

_____

Choice G: Continue living as now but take more family vacations together. Go to the mountains and ocean as much as possible.

Order: _____

Reason: _____

_____

Choice H: Plan ahead for the final months. Buy extra food, drinks, medicine, and guns for the final crazy time.

Order: _____

Reason: _____

_____

Choice I: Have the mother leave the family and go to work 24 hours a day in an astronomy research laboratory in Hawaii. Have the father go to work 24 hours a day in a computer research laboratory in Berkeley, California. Leave the children with the grandmother.

Order: _____

Reason: _____

_____

In this discussion, you will be talking about life and death. You should be very serious and sensitive. Study the following conversation expressions. Practice using them with your teacher. Then practice them with a partner. Take turns showing feelings and showing agreement and disagreement.

Showing Feelings

I feel like the family
    shouldn't do anything.

Showing Agreement

I understand how you feel,
    and I agree with you.
I know how you feel, and I feel the same way.

Showing Disagreement

I feel like the family should
    see a psychiatrist.

I understand how you feel, but I disagree with you.
I know how you feel, but I feel differently.

Continue practicing the expressions with a partner. Begin with the examples.

Example 1   A: I feel like the mother and father should quit their jobs.
              B: I understand how you feel, but I disagree with you.
              A: Please tell me why.

Example 2   B: I feel like the family should plan ahead for the final months.
              A: I know how you feel, and I feel the same way.
              B: Well, what should they do?

Study the following discussion. See how the expressions are used. Practice the discussion with two partners.

A: Well, what do you think the family should do?
B: I really don't know. It's a very difficult situation.
C: Well, in my opinion, Choice H is the best. The last six months will be crazy and dangerous. The family needs to plan ahead.
A: I understand how you feel, but I disagree with you a little bit.
C: Why? You don't think they need to plan ahead?
A: Yes, they need to plan ahead. But they don't need to buy guns.
B: I don't think so either. And I'm not sure they need to buy extra food. I don't feel like the situation will be crazy.
A: I think extra food is a good idea.
B: I know how you feel, but I feel differently.
C: Why do you feel differently?
B: Like I said. I don't think they need to buy extra food.
A: Well, let's think about some other choices.
C: Good idea, but I still like Choice H.

Discuss

This is a hard topic to discuss. As you discuss your ideas, try to listen carefully to your classmates and understand them. When your group has finished discussing the problem, share your ideas with the rest of the class.

Extend

Written/Oral Assignment

1. You have one more day to live. Write a letter to your best friend or parents (they will survive). Write about how you feel and what you will do during your last day. Share your letter with one of your classmates. Afterwards, discuss your ideas with your class.

Cultural Contact Assignment

2. Talk to your class about what to do in case of an emergency or disaster, such as a fire, a flood, a tornado, or an earthquake. Get a map of your city or town and locate all of the police and fire stations close to you.

If I Had
My Rathers

Vocabulary

solve to answer

buried put underground

Read and Consider

We have come to the last unit of this workbook. You have been asked to solve problems about green cards, ice cream, hair styles, and dinner manners.

Now it is time to think about the future. We will end the same way we began—at a party where you ask people about their opinions.

Again, you must talk to everyone in the room. Ask three questions to one of your classmates, and then move on to the next classmate.

Preconversation

By now, you are "old" friends with your classmates. Your conversation will be very informal. In this conversation, for fun, disagree loudly with your classmates. Study the following expressions. Practice using the expressions with your teacher. Then practice using them with a classmate. Take turns stating preferences and disagreeing loudly.

Stating Preferences

I'd rather spend a year in the United States than spend a year in Switzerland.

I think it would be better to spend a year in the United States than spend a year in Switzerland.

I'd prefer to spend a year in the United States than spend a year in Switzerland.

Disagreeing Loudly

Are you crazy or what?
You've got to be kidding!
You've got to be joking!
Come on, give me a break!

Continue practicing the expressions with your partner. Begin with the examples.

Example 1   A: Would you rather get a great job or learn how to speak English fluently?
B: I'd rather learn how to speak English fluently.
A: Are you crazy or what?

Example 2   B: Would you rather stay single or get married?
A: I think it would be better to get married.
B: You've got to be joking!

Study the following conversation. See how the expressions are used. Practice the conversation with your classmate.

A: Would you rather become the leader of your country or the president of a large company?

B: I'd prefer to become the leader of my country.

A: You've got to be kidding! That would be a terrible job.

B: Why do you say that?

A: Because it would be dangerous and you wouldn't have any privacy. And you could make a lot more money as the president of a company.

B: That's true, but the leader of a country has a lot of power.

A: So you would rather have power than money?

B: That's right. What about you?

A: ...

Find two people who:

1. would rather die a multibillionaire at age 60 than live to be a healthy, poor 100 year old

   _____

   _____

2. would rather have seven children than two children

   _____

   _____

3. would rather travel to Australia than to Sweden

   _____

   _____

4. would rather become ugly and happy than beautiful/handsome and unhappy

   _____

   _____

5. would rather learn how to speak Chinese and Russian than French and German

   _____

   _____

6. would rather stay single than get married

   _____

   _____

7. would rather fly into outer space than become a deep sea diver

   _____

   _____

8. would rather get a great job than learn how to speak English fluently

   _____

   _____

9. would rather go to see the next Olympics than go to the next carnival in Brazil

   _____

   _____

10. would rather win a Nobel Prize than make a lot of money

   _____

   _____

11. would rather travel around the world for one year than do what they are doing now

   _____

   _____

12. would rather become the leader of her or his country than the president of a
large company

_____

_____

13. would rather spend a year in the United States than spend a year in Switzerland

_____

_____

14. would rather live an exciting, dangerous life than a boring, safe life

_____

_____

15. would rather have a job outside their native country than inside it

_____

_____

16. would rather become a great cook than a great artist

_____

_____

17. would rather know one subject very well than know a little bit about many
subjects

_____

_____

18. would rather be frozen when they die than buried or cremated

_____

_____

19. would rather live in a penthouse in a large city than in a huge house in the country

_____

_____

20. would rather keep all the friends they have in this class than lose them

_____

_____

Discuss

Since this is the last discussion in this workbook, discuss your plans for the future with your class.

Extend

Written/Oral Assignment

1. As a follow-up to the class discussion, write a paragraph about your dreams for the future.

Cultural Contact Assignment

2. Talk to at least three Americans. Ask them:

   "Please tell me what you want your life to be like 30 years from today."

   Write down their answers and share them with the class.

Appendix: Conversational Expressions

1. Introducing Yourself
2. Responding to an Introduction
3. Meeting Questions
4. Showing Interest/Following Up
5. Preclosing a Conversation
6. Closing a Conversation
7. Agreeing
8. Agreeing with a Negative Point
9. Disagreeing
10. Partially Agreeing
11. Asking for Repetition
12. Making Suggestions
13. Asking for Reasons
14. Giving Reasons
15. Pausing While Thinking
16. Thanking Someone
17. Responding to Thanks
18. Offering an Opinion
19. Asking for an Opinion
20. Suggesting Compromise
21. Interrupting
22. Returning to an Idea

1. Introducing Yourself

Less Formal   Hi. I'm . . .What's your name?
               Hi. I'm . . .
               Hello. I'm . . .
               Hello. My name is . . .
Formal   How do you do? My name is . . .

2. Responding to an Introduction

Less Formal   Hi. I'm . . .

↑   Nice to meet you. I'm . . .

               Pleased to meet you. I'm . . .

↓   It's nice to meet you. My name is . . .

Formal   It's a pleasure to meet you. My name is . . .

3. Meeting Questions

What's your name?

Where are you from?

What do you do?

Where are you living now?

What do you like to do in your spare time?

Why did you come here?

When did you come here?

How long have you been here?

Why are you studying English?

4. Showing Interest/Following Up

Less Formal   Mmm-hmm . . . . What about you?

↑   Uh-huh . . . . How about you?

               Interesting . . . Tell me more.

↓   Really? . . . . Why? (or) Why not?

Formal   You don't say. Would you mind telling me more about . . . ?

               Could you tell me more about . . . ?

5. Preclosing a Conversation

Less Formal   OK . . . great talking to you. I've got to run.

↑   Thanks a lot for the information.

               Well, it's getting late.

               Well, I've got to go.

               Sorry, I'm supposed to be at (place) and (time). Let's get together
                 some time.

↓   Well, I'm afraid it's time to go.

Formal   Well, I wish we could talk longer, but I really have to go.

6. Closing a Conversation

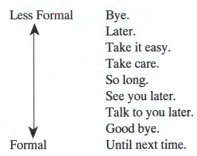

Less Formal	Bye.
	Later.
	Take it easy.
	Take care.
	So long.
	See you later.
	Talk to you later.
	Good bye.
Formal	Until next time.

7. Agreeing

Strong	You're absolutely right.
	I couldn't agree more.
	Great idea.
	Definitely.
	You can say that again.
	You're right about that.
	You're right.
	I agree.
	I think so too.
	That's a good point.
	You've got a good point there.
	Good point.
	Good idea.
	Sounds good to me.
	That makes sense.
	Me too.
	I do too.
	So do I.
	I see what you mean.
Not So Strong	That's true.

8. Agreeing with a Negative Point

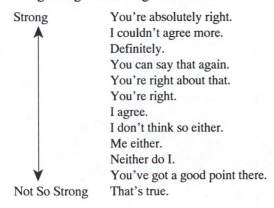

Strong	You're absolutely right.
	I couldn't agree more.
	Definitely.
	You can say that again.
	You're right about that.
	You're right.
	I agree.
	I don't think so either.
	Me either.
	Neither do I.
	You've got a good point there.
Not So Strong	That's true.

9. Disagreeing

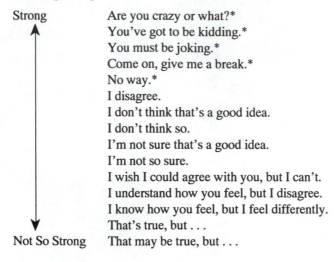

Strong	Are you crazy or what?*
	You've got to be kidding.*
	You must be joking.*
	Come on, give me a break.*
	No way.*
	I disagree.
	I don't think that's a good idea.
	I don't think so.
	I'm not sure that's a good idea.
	I'm not so sure.
	I wish I could agree with you, but I can't.
	I understand how you feel, but I disagree.
	I know how you feel, but I feel differently.
	That's true, but . . .
Not So Strong	That may be true, but . . .

10. Partially Agreeing

That seems like a good idea.
I guess that's a good idea.
I guess so.
I sort of agree.
I partly agree.
Maybe so.
Maybe.

11. Asking for Repetition

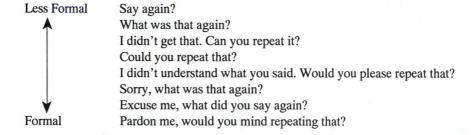

Less Formal	Say again?
	What was that again?
	I didn't get that. Can you repeat it?
	Could you repeat that?
	I didn't understand what you said. Would you please repeat that?
	Sorry, what was that again?
	Excuse me, what did you say again?
Formal	Pardon me, would you mind repeating that?

12. Making Suggestions

I definitely think that you/we should . . .
You/We should . . .
I think that you/we should . . .
I suggest that you/we . . .
In my opinion, you/we should . . .
I believe that you/we ought to . . .
I think that maybe you/we should . . .
I think that it's OK for you/we to . . .
I think that it's all right for you/we to . . .
I don't think that you/we should . . .
If I were you/she, I would . . .
If I were you/he, I wouldn't . . .

*Remember that these expressions may be considered impolite.

13. Asking for Reasons

Why?
Why not?
Why do you say that?
Why do you think that?
What's your reason for saying that?

14. Giving Reasons

Because . . .
. . . so that . . .
In order to . . .
For one thing . . .
One reason is that . . .
One point is that . . .
One thing to consider is that . . .

15. Pausing While Thinking

Let's see. I think that . . .
Let me think about that for a minute. I think that . . .
Welllllllll . . . I think that . . .
Hummmmmm . . . I think that . . .
That's a good question . . . I think that . . .
That's a tough one . . . I think that . . .

16. Thanking Someone

Less Formal	Hey, thanks.
↑	Thanks a lot.
	Thanks a million.
	I really appreciate your help.
↓	Thank you very much.
More Formal	Thank you very much for your help.

17. Responding to Thanks

Less Formal	No problem.
↑	Sure.
	Forget it.
	Anytime.
	You're welcome.
↓	Don't mention it.
	My pleasure.
More Formal	If I can do anything else, please let me know.

18. Giving an Opinion

In my opinion, I think that . . .
I think that they might/would like to . . .
I think that it might/would be interesting to . . .
I don't think that they might/would like to . . .
I think that it might/would be interesting to . . .

19. Asking for an Opinion

Well, what do you think?
What's your opinion?
How do you feel about that?
Do you agree?
Don't you agree?
Do you think that's a good idea?
You know what I mean?
Tell me what you think.
So what do you suggest?

20. Suggesting Compromise

Why don't we compromise?
How can we agree on this?
Let's look at another idea.
Let's come back to this point later.
Maybe the best thing to do is . . .

21. Interrupting

Casual

↕

Polite

Wait a minute, I think that . . .
Un-hunh, that reminds me . . .
Yeah, I'd just like to say that . . .
Sorry to interrupt you, but . . .
Excuse me, may I interrupt you for a minute?
(clear throat), umm, I think that . . .
Umm, excuse me, may I say something?

22. Returning to an Idea

Less Formal

↕

More Formal

Well, anyway . . .
Well, as I started to say, . . .
As I was saying . . .
Now where was I? . . .
Well, moving back to the subject . . .